Intrigue and War in Southwest Asia

THE STRUGGLE FOR SUPREMACY FROM CENTRAL ASIA TO IRAQ

Miron Rezun

New York
Westport, Connecticut
London

Library of Congress Cataloging-in-Publication Data

Rezun, Miron.
   Intrigue and war in southwest Asia : the struggle for supremacy
from central Asia to Iraq / Miron Rezun.
      p.   cm.
   Includes bibliographical references and index.
   ISBN 0–275–94105–1 (alk. paper)
   1. Middle East—History—20th century.   I. Title.
DS62.4.R49   1992
956.05—dc20   91–16688

British Library Cataloguing in Publication Data is available.

Library of Congress Catalog Card Number: 91–16688
ISBN: 0–275–94105–1

First published in 1992

Praeger Publishers, One Madison Avenue, New York, NY 10010
An imprint of Greenwood Publishing Group, Inc.

Printed in the United States of America

∞™

The paper used in this book complies with the
Permanent Paper Standard issued by the National
Information Standards Organization (Z39.48–1984).

10 9 8 7 6 5 4 3 2 1

To the memory of my mother—
Lea (née Kenigstein) Rezun.

Figure 1
Southwest Asia

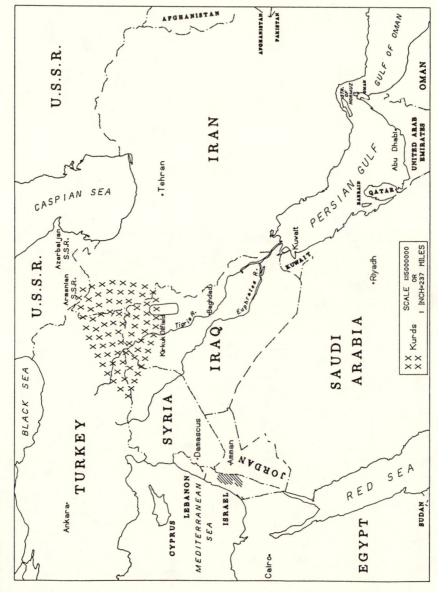

Contents

Preface

This book is written for a readership interested in what historians and political scientists call the "Great Game." The Continuation of the Great Game might have been a more appropriate title for it, to be sure, but I chose the words "intrigue" and "war" because that is what the famous Great Game was all about. It is a game of intrigue that often leads to war, retreats to some form of intrigue, and then moves on to an intriguing negotiating process aimed at achieving peace and dubious postwar settlements.

Indeed, it is my intention in this book to point out that diplomacy is essentially a gentlemanly and respectable way to conduct international politics. Diplomacy, however, is not played out on Main Street alone; one sees it in confidential meetings and in back rooms; there are often third parties who have a political stake or who want to preserve a status quo and do not necessarily become involved as the direct protagonists in a dispute or war. Naturally there are innocent victims in this international game of skulduggery. For there is much here that is simply cloak and dagger—what with international arms trade, inordinate nationalism, subterfuge, charismatic personalities, greed, vaulting ambition, and, of course, double-crossings, as well as the frequent use of the name of God, or Allah, which is usually used in vain. The media are sometimes distorted; and academics, when not excessively neutral, tend to be bigoted in their analyses. Such, in any event, is my interpretation of the "Great Game" in Southwest Asia.

This all sounds like a very pessimistic approach to what is effectively a study of rivalry and influence in a particular region of the world. Yet the study of politics may be presented in a format that turns out as dismal a science as economics; in fact, political science, and especially international politics, is not even a scientific inquiry but an art in interpreting and analyzing sociopolitical phenomena, where flawed human beings and the inexorable flow of history play such an important part. My views may also seem pessimistic to those who would prefer a more antiseptic view, one that is almost clinically sanitized, scholarly, and profoundly academic. But that would add nothing to our understanding of political conflict—it never has. As an academic, I give account for many of my arguments, but as best as I could I have tried to steer away from an unduly pedantic analysis—alas, perhaps at the risk of falling into the trap of writing too passionately, without sufficient detachment. If that is the case, then I will accept full blame for it. But the subject matter that follows in these pages is itself not bereft of an ambiguity and an emotional complexity that is difficult to evaluate with a clinical thoroughness. Even pure historical writing, based on many more sources of information, is replete with fallacies.

I must extend a heartfelt gratitude to my family for their patience with me during periods of unjustified absences in the evenings when I had to sift through countless materials. Gratitude is also extended to the Social Sciences and Humanities Research Council of Canada for a very generous grant that enabled me to travel to Soviet Central Asia, Afghanistan, Turkey, and Iran, so that I could become more familiar with the political and international processes at work in this area. I sincerely acknowledge the assistance received from Dr. Fuat Borovali of Bilkent University in Ankara, who helped me considerably in understanding the problems of the Kurds. Ms. Mary Glenn, the Political Science editor at Praeger Publishers, should be given all the credit for accepting the manuscript while still in its earlier stages. My gratitude in this respect should also go to Alda Trabucchi and Krystyna Budd, also at Praeger, for the meticulous quality control. Many thanks to go to Angela Williams for putting my rough-hewn manuscript on memory disks and to Charles Thornton, my friend and colleague at the University of New Brunswick, for making such valuable suggestions on the style and technique that helped improve the final draft.

Glossary

Abwehr—the German Wehrmacht's counterintelligence agency

al-Da'wa—underground Shi'a movement in Iraq

Amal—moderate Shi'a group

apparatchiks—Soviet term for bureaucrats and members of the Soviet Communist Party

Arab League—a group of twenty-one member Arab states

Aussenpolitisches Amt—German Foreign Ministry

Ba'athism—a political movement, strongest in Iraq and Syria, that emphasizes freedom, Arab unity, and socialism

Baghdad Pact—an alliance between the United States, the United Kingdom, Turkey, Pakistan, and Iran

Basmachestvo—the name given to the rebellion in Central Asia against the early Bolsheviks

Bazaari—small businesspersons in a *souk*

Birlik—an Uzbek nationalist movement whose name means "unity"

Brezhnev Doctrine—a doctrine espoused by the late Soviet leader Leonid Brezhnev that stated that any interference in Moscow's sphere of influence will be met with armed force

caliph—leader or sultan of Islam

CENTO—Central Treaty Organization, an organization that replaced the Baghdad Pact and involved the United States, Great Britain, Turkey, Pakistan, and Iran. It lasted from 1955 to 1979

CIA—the U.S. Central Intelligence Agency

COCOM—Coordinating Committee on Multilateral Export Controls; a part of NATO that sets restrictions on what could be sent in terms of trade to different countries

CPSU—the Russian acronym for the Communist Party of the Soviet Union

Dashnaktstiun—Armenian Christian nationalist organization

Durand line—the border between Afghanistan and present-day Pakistan

EEC—European Economic Community

Eretz Yisrael—Hebrew term for the state of Israel

Erk—an Uzbek nationalist movement whose name means "independence"

GCC—Gulf Cooperation Council, consists of Saudi Arabia, Bahrain, Oman, Kuwait, Qatar, and the United Arab Emirates. A military alliance and a union for mutual assistance

glasnost—"openness," a new political ideology in the Soviet Union

Hajj—one of the pillars of Islam, involves a pilgrimage of all Moslems, at least once in their life, to Mecca

Hizb'Allah—the Lebanese Party of God

Homo sovieticus—a mythological concept in the Soviet Union meaning "Soviet man"

Hussainiyyas—secret cells that operated in the Gulf states by Iranian secret agents

Imam—a Moslem religious leader

Intifada—the uprising by Arab Palestinians in the Israeli-occupied West Bank and Gaza Strip

Irangate—name given to a scandal that broke during the Iran-Iraq war that involved the Americans selling weapons, indirectly, to Iran in order to finance their buying of weapons for the Nicaraguan Contra rebels. Also called the Iran-Contra Scandal

ISI—Pakistan's military intelligence

Jadidism—Turkestani nationalist movement

jihad—the Islamic idea of holy war

Kadimist—a Moslem movement in Central Asia

KDP—Kurdish Democratic Party

KDPI—Kurdish Democratic Party of Iran

KDPPC—Kurdish Democratic Party Provisional Command

KGB—Soviet secret police

KHAD—former state information service of Afghanistan. See WAD

Khalq—wing of Afghan Communist Party

klassovaia baza basmachestva—Basmachi class base

Knesset—Israeli parliament

kulaks—prosperous and well-to-do Russian peasants

Kurbashi—chiefs of the Basmachi (see Basmachestvo)

Mahdi—the Moslem messiah

Majlis—the Iranian parliament

Moslem Brotherhood—founded by Hassan al-Banna; an Arab, Sunni fundamentalist movement

Mossad—the Israeli secret service

Mujahedeen—Afghan freedom fighters, or anticommunist insurgents

NATO—North Atlantic Treaty Organization

NEP—the New Economic Policy of Lenin's time

NKVD—the name for the KGB during World War II

Northern Tier—countries in Southwest Asia that border the Soviet Union, that is Turkey, Iraq, Iran, and Afghanistan

Nowruz—the Moslem New Year (primarily among the Shi'i)

OPEC—Organization of Petroleum Exporting Countries

Parcham—one wing of the Afghan Communist Party

Pax Americana—the American peace, an ideology stating what may be the new world order following the Gulf War

Pax Britannica—the British peace

PDPA—People's Democratic Party of Afghanistan, the Marxist party currently ruling Afghanistan

perestroika—economic and social reconstruction in the Soviet Union

Peshmerga—Kurdish warriors or rebels in Iraqi Kurdistan

PLO—Palestine Liberation Organization, headed by Yasser Arafat

PMOI—People's Mujahedeen of Iran

prodnalog—Soviet tax-in-kind

PUK—Patriotic Union of Kurdistan

Rastokhez—Tajik national movement whose names means "resurrection"

RDF—U.S. Rapid Deployment Joint Task Force, renamed USCENTCOM

Saadabad Pact—the predecessor of the Baghdad Pact

SALT II—Strategic Arms Limitation Talks, signed by Leonid Brezhnev and Jimmy Carter in Vienna in 1978. The United States refused to ratify in 1980

Savak—Iranian secret service under the Shah

SEATO—South East Asia Treaty Organization

Seven Sisters—a group of seven oil companies based in the Middle East

Shariat—Islamic law

Sicherheitsdienst—German (Gestapo) Secret Service

Solidarity—Polish worker's political party

Tudeh Party—Iranian Communist Party

Turan—gathering of Turkish people together as one nation

Ulema—Moslem religious leaders

Ummah—the community of Islam

USCENTCOM—American Central Command, the replacement of the RDF (Rapid Deployment Force)

WAD—current incarnation of KHAD, the Afghan secret service

Wahhabism—Sunni fundamentalist movement that started on the Arabian Peninsula

wakf lands—Moslem ecclesiastical or religious land endowments

Figure 2
Afghan Freedom fighter, armed with a Lee Enfield rifle, and his daughter.

Source: Photograph by Miron Rezun. Courtesy of Westview Press.

1

Introduction

At the turn of this century an English scholar and soldier, Alexis Krausse, a name clearly revealing some German ancestry, wrote a very interesting book titled *Russia in Asia* (1899). Even a cursory look at this thick tome suggests that Krausse believed in the greatness of the British Empire and in the mission it set out to accomplish in Asia and elsewhere. In one eloquent passage Krausse observed (consider that he was writing some ninety years ago): "The end of the growth of the Russian Empire can only be brought about by her reaching a frontier held and, if need be, defended by a nation stronger than herself." Krausse went on to say that Russia's ideal of aggrandizement was by the arts and wiles of diplomacy, not by the prosecution of war. He added that a war would seriously cripple the Russian Empire, powerful though she were, and that a war with England would spell insolvency and ruin.

In retrospect, these words have a prophetic ring. Penned by an inveterate Russophobe trying to assess the conflicting interests of the Russian and British empires, it is a story that has been told many times by statesmen and scholars in both Russia and England. Krausse was obviously worried that Britain would lose the race for Asia, or that she would be relegated in fifty years' time to the status of a third-rate power. He called Russia "one of the greatest tyrannies the world has ever known" and correctly prophesied tsardom's doom. This Englishman compared Britain to Russia as one would compare Hyperion to a Satyr: The more reflective, cerebral Englishman was contrasted with an uncivilized, war-mongering ruffian.

The truth of the matter is that Britain was fearful for her Indian empire and tried to contain Russia's southward drive while spreading her own influence northward. British and Russian intelligence agents performed extraordinary feats of espionage in their respective domains. This struggle for supremacy was dubbed the "Great Game," and that Game ended—in the opinion of some—in 1907, when Britain and Russia came to terms in the face of the growing threat from imperial Germany.

These adventures and misadventures of Russian and English heroes were recently narrated with superb skill by Peter Hopkirk in his *The Great Game* (1990). Hopkirk also ends his story around 1907, but admits that the Great Game continued beyond the First and Second World Wars, including the Cold War and the events that have filled the headlines in the 1980s and 1990s.

But what precisely was the Game all about? Where exactly was it being played? Which powers were involved then, and which powers are playing it today? What are the stakes? Has any one power ever had a clear chance of winning?

The phrase "Great Game" has in effect been attributed to Rudyard Kipling. The English author's long sojourn in India and his writings about the subcontinent gave it a certain popularized, political significance in the latter part of the nineteenth century. Its first use, however, appears to have been in J. W. Kaye's *History of the War in Afghanistan* (1857), chronicling English and Russian intrigue in that distant land. But from the very beginning the term was never confined to Afghanistan alone, as many have often claimed. The Great Game appears to have embraced the whole of Central and Southwest Asia. One story has it that a British army captain, Arthur Connolly, coined the term before he went on a mission to Bukhara (now Soviet Central Asia) in 1841. It was later said of him that he had been seized by Emir Nasr Allah (at Russian instigation?); for months he was kept in a vermin-infested pit and then was beheaded.

In fact, Britain and Russia were not the only powers playing this power game. It is difficult to imagine any area in the world where the major European powers had not become embroiled in their respective quests for extracontinental territorial expansion and political influence. Ottoman Turkey was once a half-European, half-Asian power, the so-called sick man of Europe, who could not help but interact with the Europeans. The Ottomans sought the support of the Austrians and the Germans, first to maintain control over the Balkans, and second to keep both the Russians and English from seizing their possessions in Southwest Asia. After the outcome of World War I, the Ottomans predictably lost all their possessions to the victorious European colonial powers. Indeed, throughout the twentieth century, the Great Powers have vied with one another; schemed and plotted, and at times threatened and invaded, but always left the foreign imprint on local peoples and institutions.

But where precisely is one to plot the site of the Great Game? Very broadly defined, it stretches from the border of the Indian subcontinent in the east to Turkey and Azerbaijan in the west, incorporating on the southern frontier the Arab shaykdoms of the Gulf and the land of the two rivers we have come to know as Mesopotamia, or present-day Iraq. To the northeast lie the vast Central Asian steppes, bounded from the northwest by the precipitous heights of the Caucasus and the Pamirs to the East.

It was only a decade ago that we witnessed the invasion of Afghanistan by Soviet forces. A turning point in the history of Iran came with the breathtaking upheaval of the Iranian Revolution. Iran suddenly turned anti-American. Then war erupted between Iran and Iraq, lasting eight long years and precluding any lull in the Game. When that war finally ended, Iraq settled its differences with Iran in an unlikely peace settlement and gave the Game scenario greater resonance when it went on to challenge the West in an effort to dominate the Persian Gulf. Moreover, whatever had been gestating during seventy-odd years of communist rule in the USSR suddenly surfaced as nationalist ferment in Armenia, Azerbaijan, and Central Asia, rending the homogeneous Soviet Empire asunder. For some of these phenomena there is a strong historical precedent; for others, it is contemporary history in the making. And why most of this area is so topical is no doubt due to the oil dimension. In contrast to the rest of Asia, Africa, or Latin America, for instance, the disputed areas of the Gulf are sought after and given importance because, like buried treasure, they conceal the black gold of petroleum. Lands formerly barren have suddenly acquired great economic worth.

Yet the human geography is perhaps the most important component in the rivalry. Turks, Arabs, Kurds, Armenians, Azeris, Uzbeks, Iranians, and Pushtuns make up the social landscape; at long last they are all making an important mark on their own history, each with different goals, fears, and motivations. Each is playing for stakes that are at once the same and different from those of the superpowers. One is somehow tempted to compare this story to the writing of an ancient Greek epic or tragedy, where the mythical gods on high become passionately embroiled in the affairs actually transpiring below. Conversely, the actions of smaller nations, especially in the postcolonial era, should not be regarded entirely as a function of superpower rivalry. Modern states are effectively no longer subservient to a superpower; they have an inherent imperative of their own, which often is not associated with the discretionary activity and motives of an allied power or superpower. In addition to external challenges from the West and the USSR, the Southwest Asian context can today be easily influenced by revolution, coup d'état, maldistribution of wealth, misrule and improbity, Islamic fundamentalism, and, of course, even a single charismatic personality.

When the Baghdad Pact, a Western security belt blocking Soviet expansion southward, came into existence in 1955, another term was added to the lexicon of the Great Game—that of the "Northern Tier." It was a geographic term used to denote the Moslem countries lying on the Soviet Union's southern border. Originally, these countries were Turkey, Iran, and Afghanistan, although the latter never did adhere to the Baghdad Pact, thus creating a gap in the defense line that made the slow penetration of Afghanistan by the Soviet Union that much easier.

It is often argued that the Turkey-Iran-Pakistan axis once enshrined in the Central Treaty Organization (CENTO) (the successor to the Baghdad Pact) constituted the soft underbelly of the Western defense system, compared with the relative stability of the strategic balance in central Europe and along the Sino-Soviet border. For the better part of four decades, the whole Northern Tier constituted the object of intense superpower contention.

THE FIRST MOVES IN THE GAME

No one knows for certain what the Russian tsar, Peter the Great, contemplated in writing his will. No one knows whether the tsar truly wrote one, and if he did, whether he actually left it. Yet by virtue of this document (I assume there was one) and by his other activities, history argues that Peter was motivated to transform Russia into a naval power, so that she could compete commercially with England. Success in trade and commerce required some control over the shipping lanes in the warmer seas and the possession of warm-water ports: hence the drive to the south. Peter himself temporarily wrested from Shah Tahmasp of Persia the territories of Shirvan, Dagestan, Mazandaran, and Gorgan. After him, Catherine the Great of Russia and her favorite paramour, General Suvorov, became notorious for their wars against the Turks in an attempt to reach the Bosporus and penetrate the Eastern Mediterranean.

However, it appears that the first definite scheme for an invasion of India with the object of ousting the British originated with a French nobleman: a certain A. M. de St. Génie, who submitted such a proposal to Catherine in 1791. Nothing came of the idea until 1800, when the then reigning Russian emperor, Paul, decided to embark on an invasion of India and confided the whole scheme to Napoleon Bonaparte. The half-wit tsar and the ambitious French emperor eventually did combine forces in a joint campaign. The more thoughtful Napoleon at first doubted the viability of such an undertaking; he felt it would prove difficult to supply two armies in the exhausting trek over the wastes of Central Asia and Afghanistan. But the tsar had an unbounded faith in his mission of liberating India from British rule. Besides, the French were intoxicated with military glory following their occupation of Egypt.

The inclemency of the elements notwithstanding (it was the middle of winter), the Russians assembled forty thousand men at Orenburg. A force of thirty-five thousand French sailed down the Danube, up the Don, and down the Volga to Astrabad on the Caspian. Another Russian force was to proceed from Central Russia into Khiva and Bukhara, and from there to the Indus River, while another group of French and Russian troops was to move through Persia and then toward India by way of Herat and Kandahar in what is now Afghanistan. The ill-begotten scheme fell apart when Paul's army was recalled following his assassination in March 1801.

From the outset the Game was never entirely a two-handed one, even though Britain and Russia were the major players. Following the end of the Napoleonic Wars, Central and Southwest Asia became of greater interest to the European powers as they became fully aware of the gradual weakening of the Ottoman Empire and the concomitant strengthening of the Russian Empire. Following the post-1815 realignment of forces in Europe, Germany began to show an increasing interest in supporting whichever power happened to be the weakest at any particular moment.

Although Britain's principal concern in the Great Game was India, she was not eager to see in this general geographic region the rise of any other European power. Britain was loath therefore to join with France when Russia began to threaten Turkey, a power that was no longer capable of retaining its possessions in the Middle East, let alone in Turkic, or Turkophone, Central Asia. But Britain was compelled to seek French assistance, and Russia was defeated in the Crimean War. The result was that under the Treaty of Paris (1856), Russia lost control over areas such as Kars, Wallachia, Bessarabia, and Moldavia. Although she had fared better in Persia by carving out vast territories in the north under the treaties of Gulistan (1813) and Turkomanchai (1828), the post-Crimean period was marked by Russia's turn toward Prussia, which ushered a new actor into the Game.

At first the Germans were prepared to give silent support to Russia, but after the unification of the German states under Bismarck, Berlin began to nurture designs of its own, to be pursued when and if a power vacuum appeared. In this way, the Game became a vortex of the great-power rivalries shaped by the broader interaction of all the European powers. Germany did not start to have any concrete designs until she became an ally of the Ottoman Turks and planned to extend the railroad from Berlin to Baghdad, evincing an interest in Mesopotamia and the Middle East.

As for the rivalry between Britain and Russia, the Russians decidedly were the weaker. Russia did not begin building railways in Central Asia until the 1880s, by which time Britain had constructed ten thousand miles of track in India alone. Moreover, at the turn of the twentieth century the Great Powers competed for oil resources and Britain had acquired the largest oil concession in the world, the D'Arcy concession in southern Persia—where it was possible to extract and refine cheap oil. It was the start of the largest oil company in the world at the time—what later was destined to develop into the famous BP (British Petroleum—the first of the "Seven Sisters"). Not having undergone an industrial revolution, Russia, a semi-Asiatic and semifeudal country, could not possibly compete with the developed, capitalist system of Britain, let alone confront Britain militarily with the comparatively meager material resources she possessed.

In the nineteenth century, Russia's only possible line of attack on India would have had to be through Afghanistan. There were two routes a Russian army might have followed. One would be from Tashkent and Samarkand through Balkh and Kulm to Kabul and on to India by the Khyber Pass or the Kuram route. The other would be by way of Baku and the Caspian to Merv down to Herat and on to Kandahar in Afghanistan. From that point, India would have to be entered by the Bolan Pass, a route that involved the constant fording of rivers and moving along narrow defiles, flanked by innumerable escarpments—an area impassable for at least seven months of the year. Hence Russia's underdevelopment and the topography of Southwest Asia combined to make a direct challenge to British India unlikely.

THE WATERSHED YEAR—1907

Now that we have entered the spirit of the Game, we must look at the events that led to the Russian-British entente and the treaty of 1907. A number of factors brought about a convergence of British and Russian interests and consequently an end to the first stage in the Great Game. The first was undoubtedly a far more far-sighted British leadership and the second was the changing balance of forces in Europe.

Among the many capable men who were involved in the administration of British policy in India and Southwest Asia, none was as far-sighted or as gifted as Lord Curzon. He showed a keen interest in the problems of Persia, in particular, and believed that Persia (Iran) was the key to maintaining what he faithfully called the *Pax Britannica.* In the waning years of the nineteenth century he was able to make two journeys: one in Russian Central Asia, the other in Iran. The outcome of these trips was two stout volumes—*Russia in Central Asia* and *Persia and the Persian Question*—in which Curzon outlined Russian policies of conquest directed toward the warm waters of the Persian Gulf and the Arabian Sea and, ultimately, toward India. He foresaw the need to create in Persia an effective buffer against Russian encroachment, a zone that might have to be shared with Russia to allay its appetite. In a private memorandum written around 1900, Curzon expressed the sentiment that "English policy towards Persia throughout this century has been a page of history that makes one alternately laugh with derision and groan with despair." Lord Curzon's position as viceroy in India from 1899 to 1905 gave him an opportunity to press his ideas.

Even before that, creative British and Russian diplomacy had begun to make its mark on the region, sometimes to the cost of local peoples, while to the good of the Game. In 1893, by Russian and British design, the boundary between Afghanistan and the British Empire had been defined. The "Durand line" split ethnic groups: Uzbeks and Tajiks between Afghanistan and Russia, and Pushtuns and Baluch between Afghanistan and what is now Pakistan. Both the Pushtuns and the Baluchis have since sought reunification with their brethren and the formation of autonomous enclaves. Russia and Britain were content with these divisions, however, perhaps because it gave both an opportunity to use these splits for policy advantage.

The second factor that favored a rapprochement between these erstwhile rivals was the changing balance of power in Europe that arose from the Russo-Turkish War of 1877–1878. Under the terms of the Treaty of Berlin (1878), Russia was restrained from acquiring further Turkish booty and territory by the British and the Germans. Germany now began to have a greater impact on international political events. As already mentioned, in an effort to penetrate the Middle East, Germany had started building the Berlin-Baghdad railway. This railroad was then supposed to be extended to Basra in southern Iraq and ultimately further south to what is present-day Kuwait. In England, especially, there was an awareness of the expanding German threat. The Russians, for their part, were becoming more and more disillusioned with their German and Austro-Hungarian allies over the Balkan dispute. Russia was in fact bankrupt. The tsar needed trade concessions and foreign loans to finance Russia's imperialist ambitions and to compete with the other powers. Russia could never have fulfilled the cherished dream of building railways (the Trans-Siberian and the Trans-Persian) without a substantial amount of outside support.

Russia's requirements drew France onto the scene once again. In the autumn of 1888, French bankers loaned the Russian treasury some 500 million francs, which were used to convert earlier German loans to loans with longer maturity periods and lower rates of interest. France also encouraged Russia to come to an agreement with Britain in Central and Southwest Asia. The outcome was the partition of Persia into spheres of influence, with Russia in the north, Britain in the southeast, and a buffer in the middle; there was to be no intervention in Tibet, and Britain was to have greater influence in Afghanistan. The 1907 agreement was not an alliance between the countries, merely a means of easing tension, as subsequent events would soon prove. Just three years later, in 1910, the tsarist government concluded the Potsdam agreement with Germany and acquiesced in the kaiser's project for the railway to Baghdad, in return for German support of Russian interests in Persia.

Iran (Persia) played a pivotal role in this power game. Iran is a country whose culture and language always transcended its borders. The language of the Iranian national poet Firdausi is spoken in Turkestan, Afghanistan, and Transcaspia, and Persian culture probably influenced the nations of Central and South Asia to a greater extent than has that of the semitic,

Arabic-speaking peoples to the east. Its influence is greater than that of Turkey, even though the majority of Central Asian and Transcaucasian peoples are ethnically Turkic, not Iranian. Iran is at the geographical cross-roads between East and West and, at its apogee, had been an empire builder in its own right. Iran, moreover, is endowed with incalculable energy re-sources, and this good fortune has made it the natural custodian of the Persian Gulf.

By the turn of the century Iran's oil had become a very important asset in the Game, and the companies, in addition to BP, that grew into the Seven Sisters were just then beginning to be established. At that time no oil had been discovered within Britain's possessions, and the increasing support for the Royal Navy to switch from coal to oil made British access to this resource critical. The Anglo-Persian Oil Company (the earlier name given to British Petroleum) was formed in 1908 by the British in Iran, despite pressure from Russia to prevent the granting of the concession rights. In 1913 Winston Churchill, then first Lord of the Admiralty, convinced the British government of the need to buy a fifty-one percent interest in "Anglo-Persian" to ensure the navy's continued access to cheap fuel. In this way Britain's presence in what Churchill had earlier called a vital country was entrenched, setting the scene for a time forty years later when the gov-ernment would be faced with the question of whether or not to intervene to protect this possession.

The reappearance of Russia under the guise of the Soviet Union as a power on Iran's northern frontiers infused new life into a Game that was turning in Britain's favor. Exhausted and weakened by the end of World War I, Britain was still able to cling to the status of a great power. Britain could still rely on the colonies and territories she exploited for cheap labor and cheap raw materials. Just as bankrupt Iran depended on Britain for financial subsistence, Britain depended on the oil of the Anglo-Persian Oil Company both for foreign trade and for maintaining the navy that gave her the mastery of the seas.

The Soviet Union was not even a match for Britain in a state of rapid decline. The only power capable of confronting Britain at this time was Germany. That capability, only dimly perceived in the 1920s, reached its full flowering as part of the broad Nazi challenge to the interwar order from 1933 on.[1] The pawns in this new phase of the Game remained Iran and, to a lesser extent, Afghanistan.

GERMANY MOVES ONTO THE BOARD

Initially, and perhaps ideally, Germany had hoped to reach some un-derstanding with England in regard to the Great Game. The Nazi party's foreign policy expert, Alfred Rosenberg, had in fact suggested to Hitler as early as May 12, 1934, that there should be a harmonization of British-German interests on a territorial line stretching from London to Calcutta.

Such a line, linking both our trade and air service, is dear to both the Germans and the English. When in the future we go to stake out living space for our nation, in lands between Asia and Africa, it will be imperative that we strive for the creation of a bloc of nations where the survival of the predominant and the strongest Teutonic races would be ensured. It would be necessary first of all to incorporate into this sphere the states of the Danube basin, Turkey, and Persia.[2]

Germany did everything in her power to lure Iran into its orbit. To impress the Iranians, a special decree was issued by the Reich cabinet in 1936 by which the Iranians were exempted from the restrictions of the Nuremberg racial laws and declared to be pure-blooded Aryans. Iran received all manner of commercial credits, gifts, equipment; and Reza Shah stood in awe of this display of Teutonic energy. By 1941 industry and commerce and communications and transport in Iran were run entirely by the Germans. Even the Trans-Iranian Railroad was under German control, Germany having contributed substantially to its construction; and the most important aircraft factory in the country was operated by German technicians. German agents—of both the Wehrmacht's counterintelligence agency (Abwehr) and the Gestapo's intelligence wing (Sicherheitsdienst)—swarmed into the country,[3] fostering and feeding the dreams of the Iranian armed forces for a "Greater Iran."

The outbreak of war between Germany and Britain destroyed Rosenberg's plans. Germany then turned to the Soviet Union, and on October 13, 1940, Hitler's foreign minister, Joachim von Ribbentrop, wrote to Stalin suggesting that Vyacheslav Molotov, his commissar of foreign affairs, should come to Berlin to settle once and for all the spheres of influence for the Soviet Union, Germany, Italy, and Japan. Molotov came to Berlin and, according to the German minutes captured by the Americans at the end of the war, agreed to the German proposals. When he returned to Moscow, he sent the German ambassador in Moscow, Count von der Schulenburg, a memorandum in which the Soviet Union's acceptance would imply "that the area south of Batum and Baku in the general direction of the Persian Gulf is recognized as the center of the aspirations of the Soviet Union."[4]

Both Russia and Britain were well aware of Germany's secret designs on Iran. The British were also aware that the Russians were being coaxed to fall in with the German plans. Sir Stafford Cripps, Britain's representative in Moscow at the time, repeatedly wired London to say that the Germans were pressing the Soviet Union to launch an attack on the Khuzistan oilfields. He also saw through the subtle Soviet subterfuge of going along with the Germans.[5] But it was left to Leo Amery, the secretary of state for India, to send a letter to the viceroy in India, Lord Halifax, broaching the subject of cooperation with Russia over Iran, a cooperation that did not exclude a Soviet-British invasion. Here is what Amery said:

Russia—I imagine she is really alarmed about Germany getting into Iran and will go in there first, if she does at all, with preventive intent. The question I would put to you, if there is a danger, is whether we should not deliberately do a deal with Russia over Iran, as Grey did in 1907 (or Ribbentrop did over Poland last year!), encouraging her to do what she likes in the north so long as she recognizes our interest in the south.[6]

The viceroy felt that any approach to the Russians would only show up Britain's weakness; Lord Halifax reasoned—correctly in my view—that it was always difficult to deal with the Soviet Union. At this point in the war, Britain was both weakened and weakening, and for the better part of 1940 there was more than just a little confusion at the Foreign Office and in the War Cabinet as to what to do in the event of a Soviet attack on the British in Iran. It is not difficult to imagine that if Britain had lost Iran, whether to the Germans or to the Soviets, it would have been thrown out of the Middle East and, eventually, out of India. In 1940, an Iraqi officer named Rashid Ali even staged a pro-Nazi coup in Baghdad. Like the shah of Iran, he despised the British. The British, of course, suppressed that coup. The reader of this book will realize that a careful perusal of British archival papers, including notes and memoranda to Prime Minister Churchill, indicates that the British were genuinely fearful about losing the Middle East and this was frequently voiced by the British Admiralty. It was thus not surprising that Britain and the USSR joined forces and invaded Iran the way they did in August 1941. The German invasion of the Soviet Union in June of that year gave the Russians the final impetus to work with the British in a country that offered warm-water ports and a convenient supply route for the Soviet war effort.[7]

The threat to both Britain and the Soviet Union arising from German activities in Afghanistan and India was certainly a real one. Rosenberg and the agency he headed, the Aussenpolitisches Amt, were regarded by the Germans as the authority on Eastern questions. While there were several other Nazi agencies active in the Middle East—the Foreign Office, the Abwehr, and the Sicherheitsdienst—Rosenberg was not distracted by their internecine quarrels from attempting the boldest of initiatives. He was the principal architect of a plan for Germany to advance on the USSR and India in conjunction with Afghan and Iranian forces. This operation was to take place simultaneously with the attack on the Soviet Union from the West.

For this purpose a meeting between Rosenberg, Ribbentrop, and Otto von Hentig (a Near Eastern specialist in the Foreign Ministry) had taken place in Ribbentrop's office in September 1939 to consider the possibility of staging a coup in Afghanistan to reinstate the deposed king, Amanullah. With his support, attempts would then be made to foment tribal insurrections along the Indian frontier, particularly among the Pushtuns and the Baluchis.[8] Surprisingly enough, while the Germans were discussing how they would overthrow Zahir Khan of Afghanistan, Ribbentrop sent a courier to Moscow in December of 1939 to sound out the Soviet leaders on this stage of the project.[9] They were understandably reticent about the whole matter, no doubt wondering whether the Germans entertained similar ideas about undermining Soviet interests in Iran. East German historians (before German unification in 1990) have cogently argued that these soundings in Moscow had the effect of putting the Soviet Union on guard: German intrigue in Afghanistan and Iran was viewed with grave suspicion.[10]

Events in Iran during the wartime occupation by Soviet and British forces are a tale of woe, intrigue, and grotesque duplicity. One memorable event in espionage skulduggery, not often remembered by scholars of the war, is the way in which the USSR foiled a German attempt to kill Roosevelt, Churchill, and Stalin at the "Big Three" conference in Teheran in 1943. Roosevelt admitted after the Teheran Conference that he had accepted a Soviet invitation to stay at the Soviet Embassy in the Iranian capital because Stalin himself knew of such a plot to kill the Allied leaders. After the war, Laslo Havas Mar, a French journalist of Magyar background, wrote a whole book on this subject entitled *The Long Jump*, confirming that the plot had been thwarted by the Soviet NKVD. However, many in the West, particularly in Germany, regard this as a myth, a piece of Soviet disinformation.[11]

When the Soviet army withdrew from Iran after five long years, it left behind two puppet regimes that had been set up under the Democratic Republic of Azerbaijan. Forsaken because the USSR had more urgent matters to attend to in Eastern Europe, these "states" were certainly not politically viable and collapsed early in 1947 in the first chill of the cold war. Britain had not, however, been in a position to dislodge the Soviets from northern Iran on its own. And, indeed, in quitting India in 1947, Britain began its withdrawal from the arena of the Great Game. The leading role she played so far was destined to be filled by the United States.

AMERICAN INVOLVEMENT

In seeking to consolidate the region south of the Soviet Union, the United States brought together various countries including Turkey, the United Kingdom, Pakistan, and Iran in CENTO, which lasted from 1955 to 1979. When Afghanistan chose not to adhere to the pact, United States strategy in the southwest came to focus almost exclusively on Iran.

An attempt by Mohammed Mossadeq to nationalize his country's oil and oust BP in the early 1950s was eventually met by Western intervention to topple Mossadeq and reinstate Mohammed Reza Shah Pahlavi, who had been temporarily driven into exile in the spring of 1953. The shah set out, with U.S. assistance, to make Iran the fifth power in the world by the turn of the century, and Iran became the United States "gendarme" in the Persian Gulf. The Iranian army helped the government of Oman in 1975 to put down the insurrection in Dhofar, and the shah even threatened to intervene in Somalia in 1978 when Ethiopia was about to invade that country. Iran helped Egypt, Turkey, Pakistan, and India financially—and even sold oil to Israel. The United States was allowed to monitor Soviet military activities from electronic listening posts in the north of the country.

The strong position the United States appeared to hold in the confrontation with the Soviet Union—by virtue of its ally and client, Iran—collapsed in the wake of the Islamic Revolution of 1979. There followed a long period of acrimony between the United States and Iran when Ayatollah Khomeini appeared at the helm of the Islamic Republic. There ensued a murderous war between Iran and Iraq at the end of which the United States clearly sided with Iraq. And there followed a period in which Iraq made an all-out bid for regional supremacy by annexing Kuwait and threatening Saudi Arabia. For convenience' sake, Iraq then patched things up with Iran; otherwise it could not face a far superior Western force of men and warships arrayed on its borders.

It is a contention of this book that Saddam Hussein's arrogance, his confidence, his boldness and brinkmanship, would not have been possible had the United States not actively supported him for so long. The long conflict that pitted Iran against the United States is also seen as a consequence of U.S. short-sightedness. One would even argue that U.S. moral and material support of Saddam has been greater than anything Saddam had received in the way of Soviet support for Iraqi arms. But these are all controversial, moot points that will be developed and analyzed in the chapters that follow. The major focus of this book is to detail the degree to which the Great Powers were, and are still, pursuing a never-ending game of rivalry and influence and to what extent this power struggle has been taken up by the major regional actors.

THE CHINESE DIMENSION

It is not my intention to devote any part of this book to China. China is only incidental to the Great Game. But China's importance in the region should not be underestimated. China, after all, has a common border with both Pakistan and Afghanistan. The most important piece of real estate in this multisided equation is Afghanistan's Wakhan Corridor—a narrow stretch of Afghani territory thrust in between the USSR on the north and China and Pakistan to the south. The Pamir Plateau (at a height of twelve thousand feet) is a desolate and uninhabitable region; nevertheless, the Russians claimed it as early as 1873 and sent several expeditions across the mountains to reconnoiter British positions in India. These expeditions stopped and invariably turned back after reaching the British border outposts. After some diplomatic bargaining, a joint Russo-British commission was set up to demarcate the frontier along the Pamirs. The Pamir Conference of 1895 set the final boundary between Russia and British India on the northwest frontier; essentially, the British and the Russians left a buffer zone between themselves, to the detriment of China, which did not participate in the conference. This zone—the Wakhan Corridor—was given to Afghanistan by the treaty powers. It was not until the communists came to power that China recognized the Pamir frontier settlement and laid to rest the Chinese claim to the Wakhan Corridor. To this day, China has never surrendered its claim to the Pamir Mountains.

NOTES

1. See H. G. Seraphim, ed., "England und Deutschland: Skizze einer weltpolitischen Möglichkeit," *Das Politische Tagebuch Alfred Rosenbergs 1934–1935 und 1939–1940* (Alfred Rosenberg's political diary: 1934–1939 and 1934–1940) (Munich: Deutscher Taschenbuch Verlag, 1964), 165–66.

2. See Miron Rezun, *The Iranian Crisis* (Cologne: Böhlau Verlag, 1981).

3. *Documents on German Foreign Policy, 1918–1945*, series D (1937–1945), XI: *The War Years, September 1, 1940–January 31, 1941*, no. 404, p. 715. These German protocols of 1940 were denounced as forgeries by the Soviet prosecutor at the Nuremberg trials in 1945. Yet it is doubtful that Count Friedrich Werner von der Schulenburg would have wanted to forge such a document, since he was so well disposed toward the Soviet Union in the first place and was later involved in an attempt on Hitler's life and executed. Count Schulenburg's signature is clearly appended to the relevant document at the political archives in Bonn.

4. Great Britain, F.O. 371/N 6008/96/38, no. 552, Cripps to War Cabinet, August 1940.

5. Ibid., F.O. 371/E 2692/219/34, Amery to Halifax, 23 July 1940.

6. See the diary of Fritz Grobba, *Männer and Mächte im Orient* (Men and the great powers in the East) (Gottingen: Heinemann Verlag, 1967), 186–99.

7. See my book on this subject, *The Soviet Union and Iran* (Boulder, Colo.: Westview Press, 1988).

8. *Documents on German Foreign Policy, 1918–1945*, series D, VIII: *The War Years, September 4, 1939–March 18, 1940*, no. 445, p. 521.

9. Ibid.

10. See Johannes Glasneck and Inge Kircheisen, *Turkei und Afghanistan—Brennpunkte der Orientpolitik in Zweiten Weltkrieg* (Turkey and Afghanistan—the focal points of Eastern politics during World War II.) (East Berlin: Deutsche Staatsverlag, 1968).

11. See my book *The Soviet Union and Iran*, Chapter 7, "The German Threat to the Soviet Union in Iran and the Soviet Response."

2

Basmachism: Banditry, or a Struggle between Turanian, Russian, and English Power?

Central Asian politics after the Bolshevik Revolution is a perfect example of how the Great Powers became intimately involved in regional affairs. There are parallels between what happened then and what is happening today. So before moving on to more contemporary issues, it would be useful to account for some of the contradictions inherent in Central Asia when a communist regime emerged in Russia and the Great Game with Britain was still being played out. The theme centers primarily around the Basmachi revolt against Soviet Russia.

Karl Marx once remarked that history repeats itself, first as tragedy, and thereafter as farce. The guerrilla warfare waged by the Basmachi against the early Soviet regime perhaps ought to be seen in that poignant perspective. It turned out to be less a game than a stage production. For the story of the Soviet campaign against Basmachism has all the features of tragedy and all the symptoms of a comic opera. It is a story of noble aspirations and of blighted hopes; it is a story of nationalism and of a desire for liberation that failed to secure a political foothold. It also reads like a saga of banditry and lawlessness, a romantic adventure that seemed almost destined to fulfill a great ideal.

The story unfolds in the heart of Central Asia roughly between the years 1917 and 1931, although the Soviet campaign against *Basmachestvo* (the term in Russian) is said to have officially ended around 1924. The action takes place in an area we still call Turkestan (present-day Uzbekistan) deriving from the language of the peoples of Central Asia, which is overwhelmingly Turkic, with the exception of Tajik, which is an Iranian dialect

spoken in Tadzhikistan. The Turks of Turkestan are often called Turkestanis, to distinguish them from the Turks of Asia Minor, or Turkey proper.
All Turks are ethnically kin, however, and they all belong to a nation we
call Turanian. The Turkestanis' obvious isolation—even today—from the
mainstream of Moslem culture to the south may of course be attributed
to the tsarist conquest of their lands in the nineteenth century[1] and their
incorporation into the Russian (subsequently Soviet) Empire. Turkestan
was the cradle of the Turkish race; it was the seat of a flourishing Moslem
civilization, and in its heyday it rivaled that of Baghdad and Damascus in
the East, and Cordoba in the West.

The Turks of Asia Minor began to develop the ideology of "Turan." Turan
is an idea propagating an atavistic yearning, among all Turkic peoples, for
an in-gathering of their nation under one banner. The intention is to liberate
the people from the imperialist, sometimes Russian, sometimes Armenian,
but, generally speaking, Christian yoke. There is nostalgia for the steppes
of Central Asia where their forebears, the equestrian nomads, used to roam
drinking *kimiz* (fermented horse's milk). The envisioned Turanian state
was to extend from the western reaches of the Ottoman Empire to China,
that is, from Macedonia and Thrace all the way to Chinese Turkestan. Turan
also means purging the Turkish race of Arabic, to some extent even of
Islamic influences, and returning to a pristine past unsullied by the later
acquisition of Arabic and Iranian cultures. It calls for a return to shamanic
practices, evoking the same notion of a promised land in Central Asia for
all Turks, much the same as the age-old longing for "Zion" (Zionism) among
nationalist Jews who recognized (and still do) only Palestine as their homeland.

There is a semantic note to all this. Since Turan is likened to Zion
(promised land), then "pan-Turanian" is a misnomer, because in political
terms one cannot say "pan-Zionism." Yet we can say "pan-Turkism," or
simply refer to Turanism, as an extension of all Turkic culture transcending
the boundaries of Asia Minor into Central Asia.

Basmachism was in a sense synonymous with a burgeoning Turkish
nationalist movement. But this statement comes in for further qualification.
There was a pan-Turanian nationalism, a Turkestani nationalism, a Turkish
nationalism (with its roots in Anatolia, or Asia Minor). Now the movement
called Basmachism, though not incompatible with the other three, points
up the differences between them that stand out very sharply.

Any form of nationalism at that time was considered irresponsible behavior by Moscow. Yet there were limits within which the Soviet authorities
would tolerate it, and tolerate it they did as long as they were able to
control it. However, in that it represented an insurrectionist ethic (an armed
and dangerous movement), Basmachism could not be tolerated. Moscow
even began to fear it. The tragicomic character of the story is that most
of the literature on this subject has obscured a strong distinction between

nationalism and Basmachism. Western historiography stands accused of a blatant misrepresentation of the Basmachi uprising and is responsible for glossing over the farcical nature of the Basmachi. The Basmachi movement was an anarchic Moslem uprising emerging on the heels of an embryonic Turkestani nationalist movement called Jadidism.

At this point it would perhaps be appropriate that we describe who the Basmachi really were and how they nonetheless came to play such an important role in the history of Central Asia.

The word "*basmach*" originates from the Turkic word "*basmak*," which means "ambush, raid, or attack"; the implication here is clearly someone who is a brigand, a raider, or a marauder. The accounts of most contemporaries—both Russian and Western—suggest the existence of Basmachi marauders. Brigandage was an endemic problem associated with the general decline of Turkestan. Joseph Castagné's account, one of the earliest in any Western language, tells us the Basmachi were a motley assortment of common criminals that "the Provisional Government of Russia let loose upon society by opening wide its prison doors."[2]

Soviet accounts are replete with grotesque descriptions of roving Basmachi bands notorious for terrorizing the Fergana countryside even before the Soviets came to power.[3] They lived outside settled areas in bands of thirty, sixty, even up to one hundred. The most redoubtable among them, Irgash, has been likened by Castagné to little better than a "*bandit de grand chemin*," (a highwayman). Yet by the end of 1917, with the situation in all Turkestan so confused and restless, the native peasant masses unwittingly raised them to the level of *mujahedeen*, or holy warriors, regarding them more like folk heroes.

The newly constituted provisional government of Kokand, anxious to resist the Bolsheviks, entered into parleys with their chieftains (Irgash, Mudamin-Bek, Hamdan, etc.) and invited them to form the nucleus of the Turkestani National Army.[4] The Basmachi watchword, popularized to make it sound patriotic, was "Turkestan for the Natives." Ideologically, their movement had a religious slant to it, and it was said that their struggle was waged for the defense of Islam.[5] There were particular reasons for all this, which I shall address later on.

We have many source materials to document this history. For example, eyewitness accounts by actual participants in the various phases of Basmachism for a long time constituted the best primary source. Recently, several Soviet authors began using the newly authorized archives of the Turkestan Soviet, documents that are highly selective and made accessible only to Soviet scholars.

Castagné's work—which is one of the earlier accounts—is not a memoir. His is a descriptive and, in many places, an unduly exaggerated version of the events.[6] Moreover, there appear to be only two participants in these events who lived long enough to write any memoirs. One was Mustafa

Chokai (in Russian, Chokayev) who was the president of the provisional government of Kokand, the town that first resisted Soviet rule in Turkestan and the locus of the Basmachi movement until its fall to the Bolsheviks.[7] The other was also an Eastern Turk (a Bashkir, consequently a Turkophone), who went under the name of Ahmed Zeki Velidi Togan. He was known also under his Russian cognomen, Velidov, and years before he had presided over the short-lived republic of Little Bashkiria in the Urals.

Togan had had numerous conversations with Lenin and Stalin. Eventually he, like so many others, turned against the Soviet regime and championed Turkestan's autonomy. Togan became active in Bukhara and helped organize resistance during the second phase of the Basmachi movement. He later became the confidant of the adventurer Enver Pasha, the man who instigated and led the third phase of the Basmachi insurrection.[8] After Enver's death, Togan worked closely with yet another disreputable adventurer, Haji Sami.[9] We now have substantial evidence to suggest that Togan had many times unsuccessfully appealed to the British to support the Basmachi in the latter phases of their struggle.

While the active participation of these two Eastern Turkish nationalists (their writings are copiously on record) suggests that Basmachism had a strong, intellectual leadership, that leadership, to be sure, was unsustainable for any length of time. There was only a handful of these "bourgeois intellectuals," but all of them were Russian-educated and all initially desired nothing more than some political and cultural autonomy for Turkestan within a Russian federation. Sir Olaf Caroe, digesting Togan's Turkish memoirs, argues that "Tsarist education had produced few among the Turkish or Tajik population who were able to give effect to any modern conception of the organization of a state.... The number of intellectuals among the indigenous people could be numbered on the fingers."[10] Chokai and Togan belonged to a stratum of wealthy Moslems who could not be bound by a system of tribal authority, who later despaired of their relationship with brigand Basmachi chieftains and seasoned adventurers the likes of Enver Pasha and Haji Sami.

The Kokand autonomous government itself was held together primarily by Basmachi leaders like Irgash. It was he who was named chief of the Kokand town militia. Irgash was devoid of any political purpose. Chokai, the intellectual, attests to this in the following terms: The Basmachi leaders could not "carry out a definite political programme. They were only brave fighters for whom the whole meaning of the struggle was defined by the success they obtained in the battles of the day."[11] As a result, dissension and rivalry plagued the Basmachi movement throughout, no matter who their leaders were at any given moment.

Glenda Fraser is today the foremost authority on this subject. A British-trained researcher, she has made good use of the minutes and intelligence reports compiled by the India Office and the Foreign Office at the British

Archives. If anything, these documents seem to tell us that the British authorities were not in the least interested in Turkestan's self-determination, a point of fact that Fraser emphasizes—and, curiously enough, laments—in her depiction of the latter phases of the Basmachi movement.[12] In other writings on this theme she has given a greater scope to the study than anyone else by broadening the chronology of events.

Fraser's predecessors, most of whom are in some way affiliated with the British-based Society for Central Asian Studies, a coterie of retired English civil servants from India and their younger pundit researchers, have written extensively on this subject with a pronounced British, anti-Soviet bias.[13] Nor have the eminent representatives of the Gallic idiom spared their invective for Soviet policies in Central Asia. In fact, French scholars have studied this area more than the British, but they have done a worse job of it on the whole. They romantically hold to the thesis that Basmachism was the elemental source of Turkestan nationalism of that period. Many of these scholars (Bennigsen, d'Encausse, Lemercier-Quelquejay, Broxup, etc.) have joined their English counterparts as the continental patrons of the (formerly Royal) Society for Central Asian Studies.[14]

THE SOVIET ATTITUDE TOWARD TURKESTAN

The attitude toward the Moslems of the borderlands was a mixed one. There were many decision-making centers in the USSR; there were all manner of Soviet Marxists, all kinds of ideas circulated and all of them seemed to appear at one time or another in the controversial *Novyi Vostok.* It was at once scholarly and popular and one of only two publications dealing with the problems of the East. The other was *Zhizn' Natsional'nostei.* Unfortunately, *Novyi Vostok* ceased publication on Stalin's orders in 1931. However, from the early years of the existence of Soviet Russia until that year this journal realistically documented the attitudes prevailing in the Soviet government. It was significant that the inner-Party strife in Moscow was at its height in the mid-1920s. During this period the Soviet political system allowed leading experts considerable freedom of speech and mutual criticism. Government officials, military officers, and academics enjoyed the right to express their views on issues as far-ranging as what ought to be the appropriate stand on collectivization, delayed economic development, the class struggle and the strategy and tactics the USSR needed to employ in the so-called borderlands. Thus a general philosophy within a Marxist framework was formulated in the official Soviet mind as to what to do about Turkestan and how best to deal with so dangerous a phenomenon as the Basmachi.[15]

The debates actually began well before the Soviets sponsored the First Congress of the Peoples of the East, which was held in Baku in early September of 1920. The Soviets sent a number of foreigners to this gathering: German communist, Jews, Hungarians, some Italian socialists, Italian Americans—who were of course either socialists or communists—one American romantic revolutionary—John Reed—and the elusive Enver Pasha who was a cryptic Turkic nationalist passing himself off as a great international revolutionist. Enver Pasha was one of the most important members of the Soviet delegation.

At the time, Stalin was people's commissar for nationalities, and it was Stalin's views that prevailed. Indeed, the Stalinist view—for such were not the views of all the Bolsheviks—held that the transition from a precapitalist or feudal society to that of a socialist one can be achieved. It also held the idea that in a backward area that had undergone a revolution, the system of power would have to be controlled by the Communist Party, without actually being a socialist system.[16] Such a belief was in line with the general interests of Soviet security in the borderlands, though it was not necessarily consonant with the native population's quest for self-determination. The threat to Soviet security in Turkestan, in the Soviet view, was patently the British administration in India. In purely Stalinist terms, this meant that the Soviet official attitude qualified its judgment on self-determination, upholding it in respect of foreign countries, but not in relation to the Soviet Union's border regions. Those regions might easily fall prey to the imperial interests of the Western powers and jeopardize the security of the center.

Stalin had an ongoing relationship with as famous a revolutionary as himself, a certain Mirsaid Sultangaliev, a man with whom he most likely worked in revolutionary circles in Baku before 1917. Stalin later had him purged at the height of the Basmachi revolt. Sultangaliev is generally credited with his version of what we might call a strange admixture of Moslem Bolshevism and nationalism. There is not a single Western academic who has not said something about Sultangaliev in Western historiography from Ivar Spector to Walter Laqueur to Mme. d'Encausse. All have exaggerated his importance in the politics of the region; he was important, but his influence was marginal in the USSR, mainly because he was not of Slavic stock. But who was Sultangaliev?

Sultangaliev was one of the most powerful Moslems in Stalinist times. Not only was he the highest-ranking Moslem in the Communist Party, he also belonged to a number of exclusive committees such as the Central Moslem Commissariat and the Central Executive Committee of the Tatar Republic. Sultangaliev made contact with Zeki Velidi Togan and hoped to establish a Moslem, Turanian state on socialist lines. He was very vocal about this, too vocal. By 1923 he was arrested and accused of having "nationalist deviations" (a convenient way of casting out a troublesome member of the Party). Although released, he was given the label of nationalist, which dogged his career until his final arrest in 1928.[17]

Stalin himself remarked that "if Sultan Galiev had confined himself to the ideology of pan-Turkism and pan-Islamism it would not have been so bad and I would say that this ideology, in spite of the ban pronounced by the resolution on the national question passed by the Tenth Party Congress, could be regarded as tolerable."[18] Indeed, it is felt by Indus Tahirov, a Soviet scholar who recently wrote that Sultangaliev "wanted to use the Basmachi offensive as a bargaining chip with Stalin at a time when he was becoming increasingly disappointed over Stalin's treatment of the border-lands."[19]

THE CAUSES OF THE BASMACHI MOVEMENT

As argued above, most Western analysts have pointed to the innate nationalism of Turkestan, evoking the "national consciousness" of the Tur-kestani "masses." Mimicking Chokai and Togan, they maintain that the Basmachi rising was "representative of all classes," supported both by the trading bourgeoisie and the Moslem priesthood. The Stalinist view, on the other hand, has refuted this argument from the start, namely, that a native proletariat existed in Turkestan. Even in regard to Russian Azerbaijan and the Caucasus, areas recognized as having their own industrial working class, the attitude prevailing in Moscow at the time was that a "Soviet-type system" would never really be able to assert itself unless it received the political and moral support of the Russian Soviet Federation (the RSFSR).[20] This is not to say the Soviets had dismissed the existence of a "national bourgeoisie" in Turkestan; quite the contrary, it was widely viewed in Moscow that this national bourgeoisie, or upper class, was the natural ally of the Soviet state because its nationalism was expected to be directed against the British.

From the very outset the whole Bolshevik stratagem was designed to exploit the vague religious and nationalistic tendencies of the native peo-ples, a situation that might turn to Moscow's advantage, as long as it was progressive and against the Western powers. But as I pointed out earlier, there was, strictly speaking, hardly a national bourgeoisie worthy of its name in Central Asia. One cannot imagine the sacerdotal Moslem leaders to have been the true representatives of a national bourgeoisie. Why? The clerical class was not an economic middle class. They either belonged to the upper class or they were neutral. Furthermore, they were not a bu-reaucratic class, because they did not run the government, that is, not until the advent of Khomeini in Iran. These "pious doctors in the Moslem law"[21] were the only ones who were literate (they also possessed landed property); they were capable of writing both in the local, Turkic vernacular and in Arabic (or Persian, as the case might be with a Tajik).

The Ulema (Moslem hierarchy) had no political consciousness what-soever. Neither was there any political press; there were no political parties under tsardom and no media education for the masses. The vernacular press that existed, such as *Ulugh Turkestan*, was limited in circulation, and it catered to a very restricted audience.[22] Even the ordinary *bazaari*, the craftsmen, the traders, the merchants, indeed anyone organized in a loose, medieval guild system, were commonly illiterate. The overwhelming majority of the population was not urbanized. In fact, it remained rural, or nomadic, clinging to a tribal way of life.

There was in effect some industry in Turkestan; but it was chiefly an extension of Russian entrepreneurship and commerce. The factories, mostly for cotton-ginning, considering that cotton was the only marketable cash crop in the area, were manned by Russians in the cities. And only the Russians operated railways and telegraphs. Russians (and Ukrainians) not only were settled here as peasants but made up the bulk of the working class as well. Whatever else may be true today—witness that in the 1980s and early 1990s, as I indicate in my chapter on Central Asia, there is a rapidly rising and comparatively large Moslem, indigenous population: At the beginning of this century much of Central Asia's native population was itself a minority. In the words of Olaf Caroe, "In parts of Turkestan . . . with the years, the Russians ousted the native population and attained an actual numerical preponderance."[23] Fraser graphically states that "most important and most characteristic of this process was the case of Tashkent, which, as early as 1889, had a Russian population of 20,000—forming a distinct town separate from the native city of 100,000 inhabitants."[24] Small wonder that Stalin expected the Russian proletariat in Turkestan to fulfill the historical role of revolution and of guiding the natives. When a Tashkent Soviet of workers, soldiers, and peasants was organized immediately after the October Revolution, it was exclusively European and Slavic.

But there was a Turkic nationalism in the making. There was a small intellectual class that espoused this nationalism—one that was associated with the urban areas of the semi-independent khanates of Khiva and Bukhara. It was called Jadidism, and it advocated a political nationalism based on secular and democratic values, distinct from the one that promoted a national consciousness based on the Moslem faith called Kadimist. Jadidism was originally the product of the mind of the Russian-educated Crimean Tatar Ismail Bey Gasprinskii (1851–1941). Strongly influenced by Western ideals, to be sure, Gasprinskii repeatedly tried to unite the Moslems of Russia on the basis of a common language derived from Ottoman Turkish. But he saw in Russia the role of patron and champion of the Turkic peoples. He never actually sought separation from Russia.[25]

In other writings, Gasprinskii has left us a legacy of lamentation for the past glories of Khiva and Bukhara, which had been reduced to a state of debilitation and utter ruin. "The Easterners yearn for the past, the Westerners look forward to the future" was how he would admonish his Moslem brethren.[26]

Yet on the eve of the Russian Revolution, these "Jadids" began to splinter off and, in the manner of the Young Turk movement in the Ottoman Empire, they succeeded in forming the backbone of a left-wing Jadidism that became the intellectual ferment in the khanates of Khiva and Bukhara. They rallied a group of politically minded activists, who came to be called the Young Khivans and Young Bukharans. These leftists were opposed to the emir; they despised the clerical system and advocated democratic social reforms and were ready to support the Bolsheviks. But the Bolsheviks had little use for them and treated them as typical bourgeois nationalists, to be discarded once these "oriental sympathizers" had outlived their usefulness. This is precisely what happened when the Russian Red Army took over the semi-independent khanates, astonished to find that some of the Jadidist intellectuals had joined the Basmachi bands out of sheer frustration.

But what, then, were the immediate causes that gave rise to Basmachism? Need one be educated or belong to an intelligentsia to actually feel oneself a nationalist? Most historians concur, including the early Soviet writers, who argued that it had become a mass (implying populist) movement as it gained momentum. Yet it is such a pity that Soviet historiographers have never said there was a strong racial antagonism between the Russians and the Turkestanis.[27] The fact remains, however—the typical native peasant felt he was displaced by the Russians. And Great Russian chauvinism—whether of the tsarist or Soviet hue—was still a part of the Russian mindset, particularly when dealing with non-Slavic populations. The Russians were everywhere: They operated the railways, telegraphs, and posts; they ran the banks, theaters, hospitals, schools, and newspapers. Right up until the revolution they expropriated for settlement the steppe lands used by the nomads. The Kirghiz in fact revolted in 1916 because of forced conscription into the Imperial Army for noncombatant duties. In the town of Semirechie a conflict that pitted Russian and Ukrainian settlers against Kirghiz nomads had become so violent that it put to flight one-third of the Kirghiz population to China.[28]

Then, too, there were conditions of starvation throughout Turkestan in the aftermath of the Bolshevik Revolution. Unemployment and anarchy were rife. Famine was just about everywhere in Russia at this time, so the Soviet authorities brought out the Red Army to requisition grain from the peasants. They systematically raided their *kishlaks* (small villages) to collect taxes and confiscated hoarded crops and valuables. The requisitioning and hardships were endured by all; yet in all likelihood the native population must have suffered far more than did the Russian townspeople. One-third of the Turkestanis actually died of starvation.[29]

It was against this general background that the Tashkent Soviet tried on its own to administer the whole of Turkestan under Bolshevik auspices. It made no attempt to enlist the support of the native Turkestanis, nor anyone, for that matter, who was a Moslem.[30] During the Third Congress of Soviets, convened in late November 1917, it was resolved that "the inclusion of the Moslems in the organs of the higher Regional Revolutionary Power appears at the present moment unacceptable."[31]

Many Moslem (primarily Jadidist), liberal-minded intellectuals proceeded to appeal to Moscow and the Central Bolsheviks against the high-handedness of such resolutions. More than this, the very next month (December 1917) the Fourth Extraordinary Regional Moslem Congress met in the town of Kokand and declared the independence of all Turkestan. It was a brazen act performed by a tiny group of delegates chosen from among Moslem religious leaders, Basmachi bands, and intellectuals, representing all the provinces of Turkestan. But it seemed to satisfy the needs of these groups, while Moscow, thousands of miles away, isolated from Turkestan by a civil war waged against Anton Ivanovich Denikin's and Alexander Vasilievich Kolchak's White Armies, could do precious little. The Tashkent Soviet acted on its own authority, and for more than a month the Bolshevik leaders in Petrograd and Moscow knew absolutely nothing about what was going on in Turkestan. Then it dawned on them that the Kokand autonomous government—viable or not—might pose a serious challenge to its existence. Thus, at the end of January 1918, the Tashkent Soviet pronounced the Kokand government to be "counterrevolutionary," accusing it of representing class, rather than national, interests. The Bolsheviks declared war on it and sent Red Army troops to sack the entire city and massacre its leaders. Estimates of the casualties ranged from three thousand to fourteen thousand dead. Among those who managed to flee were Chokai and Irgash. From Chokai's own account, we learn that there never was a common denominator of strategy between these two men: One was an intellectual and Basmachi sympathizer; the other became one of the legendary chieftains of the Basmachi movement after the sack of Kokand. Thus autonomous Kokand lasted only two months; obviously, without the support of Irgash and the Basmachi, it could have fallen far sooner.

BASMACHISM UNBRIDLED

When news of this episode spread throughout the Fergana Valley, it took some time for the Turkestanis to recover from the shock. And it is at this point that sympathy for the Basmachi grew to such unprecedented lengths. Their exploits against the Russians became so legendary in the love and lore of a frustrated and outraged peasantry as to make them unbelievable. The banner of revolt was soon raised by another brigand chief, Mudamin-Bek, formerly the head of the Soviet militia in the Fergana Valley town of Margelan: He was reportedly as prominent and as legendary as his rival Irgash. Before long Mudamin-Bek and Khal-Khodzha were swooping down from their mountain strongholds and attacking the villages of Russian settlers, Red Army outposts, and supply trains. As Caroe succinctly puts it, they were able "even in times of shortage to retreat to lairs in the hill country less affected by famine than the steppes".[32] Using British archival documents from the India Office, Fraser describes the strength of the Basmachi:

The total strength of the Basmachi in Fergana at this time was 1500 men under Irgash, 1200 of whom were mounted, armed with 1000 Berdan, Turkish and other rifles and 500 nondescript muzzle-loaders; 4000 men under Mudamin, 3000 of whom were mounted, armed with Berdan, Turkish or Russian rifles; and 1000 men under Khal-Khodzha.... The Basmachi sabotaged the line of various points but did not stop the traffic or keep the line out of repair. This indecisive state of things persisted until February 1920, when the Soviets launched another major offensive.[33]

Before long the Basmachi were fighting in all the districts of Fergana. Their hierarchy was very simple. The forces were loyal to a chief, or *kurbashi*, along tribal lines, and the chieftains were both administrators and feudal warlords, similar to those in China or to the Afridis and Wazirs of the northwest frontier in India. Initially they each had their fiefs in the following districts:

Irgash	Kokand to Margelan and Uch-Kurgan
Mudamin-Bek	Margelan to Skobelev, Kuva, and Assakiv
Hamdan	Andarkhan, Khodzhent, Isfara, and oil wells of Santo
Khal-Khodzha	Andizhan and Namangan
Islam-Kul	Namangan to Kara-Kul (on Syr-Dar'ya)
Ishmat Baybacha	Kokand to Besh-Aryk and toward the Karategin

Mudamin-Bek called his Basmachi marauders a "Moslem People's Army," and called for a holy war. He knew that the Moslem masses were easily fired up by vituperative statements against non-Moslems. He reasoned that religious fanaticism was better understood than the illusory concept of nationalism. So, many peasants ended up supporting Basmachism.

Soviet historians have unfortunately downplayed the native population's sympathy for Basmachism. To the masses, in a very real sense, Basmachism came to mean both icon and iconoclast; and the Basmachi, in turn, fancied themselves the heroes of the credulous and misguided masses. By the summer of 1919 the Bolshevik leadership in Moscow must have taken good stock of this state of affairs. Lenin immediately took the trouble to pen a letter on behalf of the Party Central Committee to the Tashkent Bolsheviks, pointing out the necessity of "drawing the native Turkestan population into governmental work on a broad proportional basis."[34]

One year later, amid the havoc wrought by the Basmachi that showed little signs of abatement, Stalin wrote an article for *Pravda* (October 10, 1920), in which he warned against alienating the native populations in backward areas. Quite out of character, Stalin expressly stated that "cavalry raids with the object of immediately communizing the backward masses of the people must be discarded for a cautious and well-conceived policy of gradually drawing these masses into the general stream of Soviet development."[35]

Faced with the rising popularity the Basmachi bands were enjoying, the Soviet central leadership was indeed in a quandary as to what to do. Was it to proceed with a policy of Sovietization, or was it to encourage some form of pan-Islamism to rally the Turkestan Moslems against the Western powers? The British, in the meantime, had been sending their own agents to Central Asia to appraise the situation for their authorities in India. The most notable among them was Colonel Stewart Bailey. This British officer had all along been in favor of British intervention on the side of the Basmachi.[36] The Soviet authorities suspected that Bailey was a spy, and it was customary to let foreign agents go about their business as they pleased. At the end of 1918 and throughout 1919, Moscow demanded an on-the-spot examination of the situation and sent several agents of its own into the area.[37] Thereafter several Soviet commissions were set up in Tashkent; they soon came to the conclusion that "Great Russian chauvinism" had indeed been directly responsible for the Basmachi uprising. The last Turkestan ad hoc commission also blamed the Armenian Christian nationalist organization operating in Fergana—the Dashnaktsutiun—for terrorizing the Moslem villages.[38] Another point the commission dealt with was the khanates of Khiva and Bukhara. Their semi-independent status had to be changed; they had to be brought under Bolshevik administration. Besides, Bukhara's emir had been sending guns, ammunition, and money and even giving sanctuary to the Basmachi each time they suffered defeat in the field.[39] So immediately following the surrender of Irgash,[40] the Red Army conquered Khiva and Bukhara in 1920, while the emir, still supportive of the Basmachi, went into exile. But no sooner had Irgash ceased fighting than Khal-Khodzha took over the command of his forces and joined with Mudamin-Bek, who now became the supreme commander of all Basmachi forces.

Meanwhile, Mikhail Frunze arrived in Tashkent on February 22, 1920, at the head of Red Army metropolitan troops. Frunze was a top Soviet military commander (subsequently appointed war minister after Trotsky's ouster) whose close ties to Vladimir Ilich Lenin, Leon Trotsky, and Joseph Stalin gave him full powers of decision. He came as the last in a succession of ad hoc commissions to study the situation at close hand. A plan of campaign was worked out to eradicate Basmachism in the mountains together with its remnants in Bukhara. The plan was sponsored by prominent leaders in Moscow, including Stalin and

Ivan Vladimirsky, both specialists on the nationalities question. But instead of "cavalry raids," it was decided that the coup de grâce would be better dealt by occupying whole villages, supplying the insurgent bands, and using airplanes and poison gas. Predictably, the process of Sovietization was now in full swing.

Turkestan was to be called the Turkestan Autonomous Republic of the RSFSR; and any matters relating to defense, foreign relations, finance, posts and telegraphs, the management of the economy, and the control of the Communist Party were to be under federal jurisdiction. That was considered the only way to establish a constitutional basis for relations between all the republics. The Soviet republics of Khiva and Bukhara were to be bound by similar treaties of alliance.[41]

Yet the khanate of Bukhara proved to be a particularly hard nut to crack. Eastern Bukhara especially was getting substantial support from Afghanistan. The rugged, mountainous topography of this region was a difficult one in which to conduct a prolonged military campaign against the rebels in their hideouts. The latter would usually slip across the border into Afghanistan. The fortifications the Basmachi constructed were almost impregnable, stocked with adequate amounts of food and ammunition. A makeshift workshop was built to produce their own cartridges.[42] It was to this area that the Bolshevik leadership sent Enver Pasha in the fall of 1921, having sent the former Ottoman minister for war to the Baku Congress of the Peoples of the East in September of 1920. But before discussing the misadventures of this colorful personality, it is important to point out the sudden shift in tactics the Moscow leaders had adopted.

As stated, the Congress of the Peoples of the East took place in Baku, the capital of Russian Azerbaijan. Not only did Enver attend, but Togan (Velidov) and several leaders of the Basmachi movement also came. The irony was that they came to what was essentially a Soviet-sponsored gathering while Soviet forces were at that very moment poised to invade Bukhara city. If anything, the Congress heralded a change of wind in regard to the politics of Central Asia. The New Economic Policy (NEP) of relaxation was being promulgated in all of Russia and was beginning to affect Central Asia as well. For instance, the grain requisition gave way to the *prodnalog* (tax-in-kind), relieving a tremendous onus on the Turkestani peasant. Trade between Turkestan and Central Russia resumed, local markets and bazaars were reopened, and the ban on private trading was lifted. The *Shariat* of the faithful was no longer slurred, and the property rights of the rich Moslem *kulaks* were henceforth respected. Everything that had been confiscated in the revolution from the Moslem priesthood (i.e., *wakf* lands) was promptly given back. No doubt by making all these concessions to the inhabitants of Turkestan, the Bolsheviks had regained some of their lost prestige.

A SONG OF HEROES, SCHOLARS, MAVERICKS, AND ADVENTURERS

Sultangaliev, Zeki Togan, Enver Pasha, Haji Sami, Sher Mohammed, Ibrahim-Bek—and a score of others, too numerous to mention—were all instrumental in Basmachism. The ones listed above were prime movers. Vaulting ambitions were behind their inveterate villainy, their unrepentant fanaticism, and their foolhardy dreams. None achieved fulfillment.

One of the two who was left alive to tell his one-sided story turned out to be an egregious academic. Regrettably, Soviet historians have been uncannily (but understandably) silent about Enver Pasha's role when he was an agent for the Soviet side. The Soviets likewise were taciturn about the activities of Haji Sami, and their almost total neglect of Togan (the academic) as an element in the skein of their narration is as revealing in its silence as it is in its admissions. Surprisingly, the least important, but one who by their own accounts seems to have caused the most problems, is Ibrahim-Bek—a laconic brigand whom they were not able to capture until 1931. Certainly a serious and sober account would not be a full one if it did not recount the bold and sad saga of Enver Pasha. At once a tale of tragedy and derision, Enver's appearance on the Central Asian scene, more than Sultangaliev's, is what ultimately, and dramatically, alerted the Soviet leadership to the seriousness of the whole insurgency.

Enver was the son-in-law of Sultan-Caliph Mehmet Reshad (Mahomet V, 1909–1918) and had been war minister of the Ottoman Empire from 1913 to 1918. After Turkey's defeat, he fled to Germany and remained implacably opposed to Kemal Ataturk and the new regime in his homeland. The Turks considered him an outcast and sentenced him to death *in absentia.* By the Western allies he was regarded as a war criminal for participation in the Armenian and Bulgarian atrocities. From Berlin he entered into protracted negotiations with Karl Radek (a Polish Bolshevik, and a favorite of Lenin) and was finally given an invitation to come to Moscow to meet with Lenin and the other leaders.

The Soviets felt strongly that the Sovietization of Turkestan required some pan-Islamic overtones; otherwise, it would be difficult to administer it. Enver, as an outspoken opponent of the British Empire, was designated as the best link in that would-be Soviet-Moslem alliance. What long-term goals they had for Enver will never be known. Whether or not they actually trusted him to promote Bolshevism in Turkestan is in itself a moot question.[43] But he certainly served their purpose when they sent him to Baku for the Congress of the Peoples of the East. In any case, Enver was never sympathetic to Bolshevism, and his arrival in Baku seems to have been a mere pose. His real aims lay in pan-Turanianism and pan-Islamism. Enver was every bit a romantic, imbibing himself with the mystical dreams of certain young Turks regarding the home of the Turks. He believed in the possibility of reinvigorating the whole Turkic race, and he desperately tried to reach what to him was actually Turania, which to others, of course, had always been Turkestan. One observer eloquently put it in this way: "And in order to reach his goal, he even went so far at the Baku Congress of Peoples of the Orient as to slam on his head the Phrygian cap of proletarian revolution."[44]

Together with a retinue of seventy-four ex-Turkish officers chosen as his military staff, Enver came to Turkestan to enlist Moslem troops for the Soviet cause. His orders were to take prompt military action against the rebels led by the ex-emir of Bukhara and his indefatigable tribal commander, Ibrahim-Bek. The most prominent member of Enver's staff was a man of the same ideological mold named Haji Sami. Now here is the irony: From the very moment of his arrival in Turkestan, Sami and the entire cohort suddenly defected to the Basmachi. There is some evidence to suggest that the defection was planned in advance but engineered by Haji Sami and Zeki Togan (who must have come before him to Turkestan), either during Enver's stay in Tashkent or while he sojourned in Samarkand. Moreover, Togan had by this time become head of a secret organization called the Turkestan Nationalist Union.[45] But just who, or what, foreign power was financing this organization? The answer is uncertain. Soviet historiographers characteristically point to England.

From evidence that is so far available, this does not appear to be so; perhaps some anti-Kemalist groups in Turkey were in on it; perhaps even the Kemalist government itself was financing Haji Sami.[46] Whatever the case may be, no sooner did Enver arrive in Bukhara than the Bolsheviks began to suspect him of sinister dealings. When they instructed him to return to Moscow under escort, he threw in his lot with the Basmachi and immediately set out to visit their strongholds in Eastern Bukhara.

Upon his arrival in Eastern Bukhara, Enver was ordered arrested by Ibrahim-Bek and was not set free until the ex-emir, Seid Alim Khan, intervened and made him the commander-in-chief of all Basmachi forces. Enver is said to have accumulated as many as fifty thousand men under his command,[47] a figure that, in hindsight, is likely to be grossly exaggerated. The only significant success he had was the capture of Dushanbe in the heart of present-day Tadzhikistan. There, reportedly, he acquired 120 rifles and two machine guns, and successfully rallied some, not all, Basmachi chieftains to his side. The big names were Sher Mohammed in Fergana; Atshil-Bek, who was *kurbashi*, in the area of Samarkand; and Osman-Bek in the region of Khiva, including some arms and three hundred volunteers from Afghanistan. Among the others, the most notable was Ibrahim-Bek, who, always distrustful of Enver, stood aloof and took no part in any of Enver's campaigns.

Enver had absolutely no artillery, and he insisted on fighting the Red Army forces in conventional, open battles rather than relying on guerrilla tactics. Nor was he able to get assistance from the British in India in view of his past intrigues. The Basmachi troops, composed of Uzbeks, Tadzhiks, and Bukharans, had rifles but had to capture ammunition they did not have or did not carry with them. Even Zeki Togan wrote to him from Bukhara City suggesting it would be better to retire to Afghanistan, since the Soviets had planned to bring 100,000 troops into Turkestan under Marshal Budyennyi.[48] It was no secret in Bukhara that Sergio Ordzonikidze, an influential Georgian Bolshevik and member of the Soviet Politburo, would soon arrive from Moscow to take stock of the situation. The campaign against Enver did not require huge formations; in one column there were 2,800 infantry, 1,200 cavalry, and twelve pieces of artillery; the other column had 1,700 infantry, 1,000 cavalry and eight field guns. There was also a Soviet Tatar brigade of roughly 8,000 men. But, even though hopelessly outgunned, Enver had no qualms about sending a tersely worded ultimatum to the Soviet government, calling for the withdrawal of Bolshevik forces (approximately 196,000 at the time) from Turkestan and declaring the independence of the Moslem peoples from the Russian yoke.[49] The Soviet government sent no reply to this ultimatum; it merely issued a statement, with tongue in cheek, that Enver Pasha "is an agent of British Imperialism".[50] On June 15, 1922, Red Army forces defeated him at the battle of Kafrun; and on August 8, during a minor skirmish, he and his company were cut to pieces. Here is the best account of that engagement:

The vanguard of the enemy occupied a mound at the kishlak of Obi-Dara, (12 versts north-east of Bal'dzhuan), and consisted of up to 500 cavalry. The 15th cavalry regiment was sent to cut off the escape of the enemy. The 16th cavalry was ordered to attack from the front. Squadrons of the regiment surrounded the mound. The first squadron making a frontal attack had to hasten because of the steepness of the slope. Despite the difficulty of movement and losses, they moved forward attacking vigorously. Enver Pasha, finding himself confronted by the advance detachment, gathered around him about 100 horsemen and decided to cut through the lines of the oncoming squadron. Rushing downhill he routed the first squadron and set upon them as they retreated. Absorbed in this pursuit he fell under the fire of the third squadron, and was killed outright, receiving five wounds. With him perished his companion-in-arms Davlet, who rushed to his aid.[51]

That was the end of Enver's aborted epic, a confirmation "of the loneliness of his political credo," for, at bottom, he was something of an interloper. One need not look further than the fact that as a Western Turk, Enver never really became popular in Central Asia.[52]

But with Enver gone, Haji Sami carried on with the fragmented leadership. Alias Salim Pasha, agent of the English secret service according to the latest Soviet version,[53] Haji desperately tried to regroup the defeated Basmachi. He concealed the news of Enver's death (except from Zeki Togan) and went about appealing for more recruits while circulating bogus papers signed by Enver. The Soviets saw through this subterfuge and, to gain some respite to recruit more Moslems into the Red Army, they began to parley with Sami. The British did not catch on to this (nor to Enver's death, for that matter) until early 1923, when the India Office became concerned about the creation of a Moslem confederacy in Turkestan, a spark that might ignite a revolt in Moslem India. To the British, Sami, like Enver, had been responsible for atrocities perpetrated against Armenians, Bulgarians, and the English. One official memo in the British Foreign Office described Sami as a man who had "played almost every conceivable disreputable part in Turkish politics for the past 25 years.... He was a jackal and a villain of the deepest dye."[54]

We now know that neither of these Basmachi leaders was an outright agent in the pay of the British; however, Haji Sami and Zeki Togan did try, in every which way, to enlist British support. In Meshed, Togan appealed on Sami's behalf to the British military attache, Major S. Thompson, optimistically predicting that with the necessary wherewithal one could automatically expect a general uprising and defections from the Red Army in Turkestan.[55] It was not long before Sami himself, after fleeing to Meshed, appealed to Major Thompson. Five thousand Basmachi were still fighting in eastern Bukhara, he said, and warned that the Soviets were anxious to invade Afghanistan.[56] Meanwhile to maintain a modicum of leadership among the Basmachi rebels, he promised them that British and Afghan military assistance was forthcoming.

The British wanted nothing to do with fugitives from Turkestan, and certainly not with the likes of Haji Sami. King Amunnulah Khan of Afghanistan had signed a treaty of friendship and nonaggression with Soviet Russia in 1921 and was therefore reluctant to help the lost cause of Basmachism. An interesting sidelight to this episode occurred when the ex-emir of Bukhara appealed to the League of Nations, charging that his land and people were being trampled underfoot by the Red Army; but the British Foreign Office tried to stifle the document.[57] Nor did Kemal Ataturk nurture anything but contempt for Enver and Sami; after all, both of them intended to kill the Turkish leader. Although Kemal may or may not have been a distant party to their pan-Turanian ambitions, it was the Kemalist secret police, under Kemal's orders, of course, that ultimately trapped and shot the treacherous Haji Sami. He had defected to, of all people, the sworn enemies of the Turks, the Greeks.[58]

From then until its demise in 1931, Basmachism became both erratic and sporadic. Ibrahim-Bek remained the elusive chief protagonist. But it could no longer marshall the support of the native masses the way it once did, relapsing into exactly what it started out as in the first place—pure banditry. But why did it resurface after 1923?

The NEP years of relaxed economic pressure were drawing to a close, and Stalin's program of "socialism in one country" was synonymous with

quasi-coercive methods of rapid industrialization and the total collectivization of agriculture. It was a difficult period in the history of the USSR,
and certainly no less, and perhaps even more so, for Central Asia than it
was for European Russia. Many Turkestani peasants were reluctant to be
forced into collective farms. There were poor, landless peasants and there
were the well-to-do peasants as well. All seemed to be attracted to these
Basmachi, who represented their only pillar of support. For this reason, it
is not surprising, for a brief period, that there appeared an uncritical acceptance of Basmachism's spurious ideology.

At a loss as to what to do, the communist bureaucrats were quick to
ascribe to it a "class base" (*klassovaia baza basmachestva*). The authorities
found it convenient to wrap explanations in Marxist terms, for it was useless
to simply call them bandits all the time. Like a recurring pattern the Basmachi attacks continued to center on the Afghan-Tadzhikistan frontiers,
allowing the bands to escape across the Afghan border after each defeat.
Two large and secret Basmachi conferences were held, almost in the manner of an American Indian powwow, sponsored by the ex-emir of Bukhara
and headed by Ibrahim-Bek. Naturally Soviet historians had wrongly believed that these meetings were organized by the British secret service,[59]
in the same way that they have correctly assumed that King Amanullah
Khan of Afghanistan was deposed in 1929 as a result of British pressure
and intrigue. That year, in fact, saw the first Soviet invasion of Afghanistan
by a very sizable Red Army contingent. It withdrew only when the rebels
had dispersed deep inside Afghanistan. With the capture of Ibrahim-Bek,
Basmachism became a thing of the past, until late 1979, when another form
of Moslem insurgence appeared to shatter that myth.

The Soviet campaign against the Basmachi was a memorable experience
in the tactics and strategy of Bolshevik Russia in the peripheral areas.
Basmachism was just one among many of the frustrations that sprung from
the upheaval of revolution and civil war. In a very real sense, when reflecting
on the Basmachi movement, one is drawn to the reverberations caused by
the Soviet invasion of Afghanistan; perhaps, too, one might see some similarity with events in the Islamic Republic of Iran. But there also that
similarity promptly ends when examined on a deeper level. The Soviet
Central Asian republics are today far more developed than either Iran or
Afghanistan, and they are culturally further ahead than any Arab Moslem
country as well.

The southern frontier was vital because it lay opposite a vastly superior,
though by no means more influential, British power in India and in the
Persian Gulf. There was chaos and ruin in these borderlands that required
immediate attention. Instead, the newly constituted Soviet authorities only
aggravated matters by their high-handed manner in dealing with the native
peoples of Turkestan. To resist Soviet hegemony, Basmachism appeared
to hold the answer to all the problems of the disgruntled elements of the

population. Yet it hardly raised itself to represent an organized native national movement; it was bereft of any political content, except perhaps that of race. Its leaders resorted consistently to pillage, brigandage, and a spoliation of the resources of a developing economy. Paradoxically, Basmachism was also intermittently supported by a native peasantry who knew at the same time that it was supporting brigands and tribal marauders. Certain intellectuals knew this as well, but they tried nevertheless to give the whole eclectic movement a political direction.

The struggle was uneven from the very start. The Red Army surpassed the bands of Basmachi in everything from numbers and training to military equipment. Despite the resourcefulness of the Basmachi, Soviet troops were, by 1930, able to kill hundreds of these tribal warriors with airplanes and automatic weapons. After almost each engagement—most of which took place in Fergana and in eastern Bukhara—the Red forces were essentially involved in mopping-up operations. The surviving *kurbashi* leaders—Ibrahim-Bek, Djunaid-Khan, Kuram-Bek, and many others—fled to Afghanistan, and most of the fighting from 1929 to 1931 was the result of Basmachi attacks led from across the border by Ibrahim-Bek. Over 200,000 Turkestani inhabitants had fled to Afghanistan by the end of the campaign, and only 33,000 of these refugees returned to Tadzhikistan in the Soviet Union. Many of the partisans resisting the Soviet-backed regime in Kabul in the 1980s were the direct descendants, not of the Basmachi, but of these refugees.

The Basmachi rebels themselves shared two important drawbacks: First, they suffered commonly from a (congenital?) inability to work together; second, they were led by either bandits or self-seeking opportunists. Suffice it to say that rivalry and dissension among the Basmachi was proverbial, similar to that among the Afghan guerrillas many years later. In the first phases of Basmachism, Irgash competed with Mudamin-Bek for supremacy in the Fergana Valley after the fall of Kokand. Then, when Irgash and Mudamin-Bek surrendered to Bolshevik forces, with Mudamin-Bek effectively co-opted into becoming the military prefect of the Namangan area, the Soviets sent him on a peace mission to another Basmachi chief, Sher Mohammed, who shot him. Further dissension arose when dual leadership had to be shared between Sher Mohammed and the Kirghiz Muetdin. Sher Mohammed would recruit Uzbeks while Muetdin would recruit Kirghiz. The Soviets exploited this duality by stealing or poisoning Kirghiz cattle and blaming it on the Uzbek Basmachi. They would then hang portraits of Lenin in a mosque or kidnap an Uzbek Basmachi supporter and attribute such incidents to the Kirghiz. In the third phase of Basmachism, under the leadership of Enver Pasha, almost all the Turkestanis became extremely suspicious of him. They avoided Enver—as did the ex-emir of Bukhara. Ibrahim-Bek actually had Enver arrested until the ex-emir intervened. Enver's successor in the fourth phase of the movement, Haji Sami, was distrusted by all the Eastern Turks, as opposed to the Western Turks, because he had promised them British military support and failed to make good on that promise. In general, Western Turks and Eastern Turks never got along, except for Zeki Togan, who in this whole story plays the part of an *eminence grise*; in maverick-fashion, he is the only one who escapes with his head intact, retiring to Turkey and becoming, for posterity, the omniscient professor of Turanian history at the University of Istanbul.

One final remark is in order. Only foreign intervention or foreign military assistance might have saved or at least prolonged the struggle of the Basmachi. But Britain clearly abdicated that role. Britain had her own Basmachi-type rebellions to worry about in the Moslem and Punjabi areas of India, so London was reluctant to come to the assistance of what many British policy makers considered to be the lost cause of simple bandits. This afterthought might explain how Soviet observers would later view the continuation of the Afghan resistance movement, which, strangely, Moscow also referred to as the Basmachi.

NOTES

1. For example, the Russians captured Tashkent in 1865, Samarkand in 1868, Khiva in 1873, and Kokand in 1876.

2. Joseph Castagné, *Les Basmatchis* (The Basmachi) (Paris: Editions Leroux, 1925), 12.

3. Iurevitch A. Poliakov and A. I. Chugunov, *Konets Basmachestva* (Moscow: Nauka, 1976), 24–25.

4. Castagné, *Les Basmatchis*, 14.

5. See *Novyi Vostok* (The New Orient), vol. 3 (1922), 37. See also A. Park, *Bolshevism in Turkestan, 1917–27*, 34.

6. Castagné was a French archeologist working in the Fergana district during 1918 and 1919.

7. Mustafa Chokai, *Turkestan pod Vlastiu Sovietov* (Turkestan under Soviet power) (Paris: Izdatel'stvo 'Pravda,' 1935). For a succinct English-language account, see Mustafa Chokayev, "The Basmachi Movement in Turkestan," *Asiatic Review*, vol. 24, no. 4 (1928), 280–83.

8. In 1929, Togan settled down in Turkey to write his monumental work *Bugünku Turkili* (Turkestan Today) (Istanbul: Cumhüriyet, 1942). Olaf Caroe, *Soviet Empire: The Turks of Central Asia and Stalinism* (London: Macmillan and Co., 1953), has based this book almost exclusively on his readings of Togan in Turkish.

9. This evidence is not Togan's but Glenda Fraser's. See her "Haji Sami and the Turkestan Federation," *Asian Affairs*, vol. 28, pt. 1 (1987), 17.

10. Caroe, *Soviet Empire*, 97.

11. Chokayev, "The Basmachi Movement in Turkestan," 281.

12. Fraser, "Haji Sami and the Turkestan Federation," 11–21.

13. For many years their violently anti-Soviet views have predominated: Colonel Wheeler, Enders Wimbush, Marie Broxup, Milan Hauner, the late Alexandre Bennigsen.

14. There appears to be an exception in the person of Hélène Carrère d'Encausse—no less anti-Soviet, but probably the world's most published Sovietologist to date. One of her earlier works, relating to the present subject is *Réforme et Révolution chez les Musulmans de l'Empire Russe: Bukhara, 1867–1924* (Reform and revolution among Muslims of the Russian Empire) (Paris: Armand Colin, 1966), 312 pp. For a more detailed account of contemporary Western writings on Central Asia, see Miron Rezun, "The Soviet Moslems: A Re-assessment," *Middle East Focus*, vol. 9, no. 4 (Spring 1987), 10–15. Other writers wrote in German. This was the case of Baymirza Hayit, an Uzbek major in the Soviet army who defected to the Germans in World War II. He was also on the editorial board of the British Society for Central Asian Studies. See Baymirza Hayit, *Turkestan in XX Jahrhundert* (Turkestan in the 20th Century) (Darmstadt: Droste Heinemann, 1956).

15. See Miron Rezun, *The Soviet Union and Iran: Soviet Policy in Iran from the Beginnings of the Pahlavi Dynasty until the Soviet Invasion in 1941* (Alphen aan den Rijn: Sijthoff and Noordhoff, 1981), 40. Reissued by Westview Press in 1988.

16. Ibid., 19.

17. Azade-Ayse Rorlich, "The Disappearance of an Old Taboo: Is Sultangaliev Becoming Persona Grata?" in Radio Liberty, *Report on the USSR*, September 29, 1989, p. 16.

18. Quoted from the text of a speech published in Alexandre A. Bennigsen and S. Enders Wimbush, *Muslim National Communism in the Soviet Union: A Revolutionary Strategy for the Colonial World* (Chicago: University of Chicago Press, 1979), 161, as quoted in Azade-Ayse Rorlich, "Disappearance of an Old Taboo," 18.

19. Ibid.

20. Ibid., 32–33.

21. Caroe, *Soviet Empire*, 97.

22. Glenda Fraser's is the latest account pointing to this distinct deficiency in vernacular sources of information. See Glenda Fraser, "Basmachi—I," *Central Asian Survey*, vol. 6, no. 1 (1987), 9. (This is the official journal of the British Society for Central Asian Studies.)

23. Caroe, *Soviet Empire*, 143.

24. Fraser, "Basmachi—I," 1.

25. Ibid., 12.

26. From Gasprinskii's Arab-language *al-Nàhda*, no. 1, p. 3 (column *e*), as quoted by Thomas Kuttner, "Russian Jadidism and the Islamic World," *Cahiers du Monde russe et soviétique*, vol. 3–4, no. 16 (July-December 1975), 397–99.

27. Glenda Fraser is of this view. Recent writings by Tatars in the USSR, in the spirit of *glasnost*, have pointed to the fact that Stalin hated Tatars.

28. Serge A. Zenkowski, *Pan-Turkism and Islam in Russia*. Trans. by Betty Jean Zenkowski (Cambridge: Harvard University Press, 1958), 134.

29. Turar Ryskulov, *Revoliutsia i Korennoe Naselenie Turkestana* (Revolution and the native population of Turkestan) (Tashkent: 1925), quoted by Park, *Bolshevism in Turkestan*, 39.

30. The Tashkent Soviet acted in the same manner as did the Turkestan Committee before it which represented Alexander Kerensky's provisional government. It excluded all Asians.

31. Chokayev, "The Basmachi Movement in Turkestan," 406.

32. Caroe, *Soviet Empire*, 101.

33. Fraser, "Basmachi—I," 30.

34. V. I. Lenin, *Sobranie Sochineniia* (Works) 2nd ed. (Moscow: Politizat, July 1919, p. 361).

35. Josef Stalin, *Sochineniia*, (Works) vol. 4, (Moscow: Politizat, p. 362).

36. For a full account, see F. M. Bailey, *Mission to Tashkent* (London: J. Cape, 1946).

37. Fraser, "Basmachi—I," 28.

38. A. I. Zevelev, Iu. A. Poliakov, and A. I. Chugunov, *Basmachestvo: Vozniknovenie, Sushchnost', Krakh.* (Moscow: Nauka, 1981), 218.

39. Ibid., 81.

40. For Irgash's exploits and his fortifications at Kara Kalpak, see Fraser, "Basmachi—I," 27.

41. For the agreements between Khorezm (Khiva), Bukhara, and the RSFSR, see Leonard Shapiro, ed., *Soviet Treaty Series: A Collection of Bilateral Treaties, Agreements and Conventions*, etc. *Concluded between the Soviet Union and Foreign Powers* (Washington, D.C.: U.S. State Department, 1950) I., Khorezm 59–60, Bukhara 98–100. In the case of Bukhara, the RSFSR undertook in a subsequent agreement the "armed protection" of the Bukharan-Afghan customs frontier and subordinated the border guards to the Turkestan Military District.

42. Zevelev, Poliakov, and Chugunov, *Basmachestvo*, 86.

43. Present-day Soviet historians say that he was an "*angliskii stavlennik*" (a British stool-pigeon). See the chapter on Enver Pasha in ibid. When recruiting him, the Bolsheviks never put him in the same respectable category as the Indian communist M. N. Roy.

44. H. Mantsoruddin Almad, *Kampf um leere Räume, Turan-Turkestan-Tibet* (Moscow: Nauka), and in Hayit, *Turkestan in XX Jahrhundert*, as quoted by Fraser, "Basmachi—I," 55.

45. See Fraser's account, which is derived from British Intelligence reports, in "Haji Sami and the Turkestan Federation," 12.

46. Fraser, "Basmachi—I," 64, which is also based on a British Intelligence report for the India Office.

47. Zevelev, Poliakov, and Chugunov, *Basmachestvo*, 114.

48. Fraser, "Basmachi—I," 59.

49. Zevelev, Poliakov, and Chugunov, *Basmachestvo*, 114.

50. Fraser, "Basmachi—I," 59.

51. Kozlovskiy, *Krasnaia Armiya v Srednei Azii* (The Red Army in Central Asia), 53.

52. Azade-Ayse Rorlich, "Fellow Travellers: Enver Pasha and the Bolshevik Government 1918—1920," *Asian Affairs*, vol. 13, no. 3 (1982), 294–95.

53. Zevelev, Poliakov, and Chugunov, *Basmachestvo*, 124.

54. Quoted by Fraser in "Haji Sami and the Turkestan Federation," 19.

55. Ibid., 17.

56. Ibid., 18.

57. Ibid., 20.

58. Ibid., 19.

59. Zevelev, Poliakov, and Chugunov, *Basmachestvo*, 160.

3

Afghanistan: The Perennial Quagmire

In Afghanistan everything appears to be at once more simple and more complicated than it is in Iran. A far poorer, far less populated and a far less developed country (most of which is rugged and impenetrable) suggests that Afghanistan should not command too much of our attention. Like Iran, except that it is land-locked, Afghanistan represents a strategic land bridge between east and west. Afghanistan has never been a colony of the imperial powers that sent armies to conquer it, at least not for any long duration.

Because of its relative backwardness, Afghanistan has never had a tradition of central government control and administration. Whatever central authority existed in the capital, such power was never able to hold much sway over the countryside, either for the collection of taxes, the imposition of legislation in the villages, or the establishment of amenities and services that are the basic ingredients of modern statehood. Afghanistan is one of the most undeveloped places in the world, where the recalcitrant behavior of independent tribes has often been condoned or gone unnoticed by Kabul, the capital. Feudal peasants rarely see the world except in terms defined by strict tribal loyalties. Many languages are spoken: Pushtu, Tadzhik, Dari, Farsi, Baluch, Uzbek, Turkoman, and so on; the dominant tribal group is the Pathan, or Pushtun—which has always been the most volatile. The rural areas are strongly bound and influenced by a rigid, Sunni Moslem fundamentalism, not as expansive perhaps as in Iran, but just as pervasive, and in a constant state of anarchy.

Afghanistan, moreover, had always defied the most elementary notions of kingship. Yet as far back as 1747, a twenty-four-year-old Pushtun (or Pathan) from the dominant tribal group had in fact attempted to forge together an "Afghan" nation out of the mosaic of tribes and languages. His name was Ahmad Shah, and he did successfully, and in a sense legitimately, establish the Pushtu "Durani" line of kings. It was this line that governed the country until the deposition of Zahir Shah in 1973 and the Afghan communist coup d'etat that followed in 1978. Until then, the Durani kings governed in their own names; they maintained themselves in power, as best they could, and for the most part, when not dependent on the Pathan tribe, answered to either Britain or Russia.

As I indicated in my introductory chapter, the Great Game did not really get underway until about the middle of the nineteenth century, when Britain and Russia began to take notice of each other in Persia and Afghanistan. The story is often told of the governor general of India Lord Auckland's inordinate suspicions of tsarist Russia. Lord Auckland set about replacing King Dost Mohammed in Kabul with Amir Shah Shuja-ul-Mulk; for the British did not regard Dost Mohammed as a trustworthy ally. The British-Indian administration in Kabul got its way in August 1839. But no sooner had the British restored their man to the throne than an open tribal rebellion erupted. Rioting Afghans stormed the home of the British resident in the Afghan capital and hacked him to pieces.[1] Unwilling to conduct a war at this time, the British concluded a treaty in 1841 and, in early January 1842, began what turned out to be a tragic trek back to India.

A total of sixty-five hundred British soldiers retreated across the forbidding, snow-swept mountain passes in one long, lazy column toward the Khyber Pass. Only a single survivor, a medical doctor on horseback, reached the Jalalabad fortress alive. All the others were treacherously slaughtered on the way. The British had been deceived. Prior to their withdrawal, they managed to secure safe passage out of Afghanistan if they left the country and allowed the former king to return. From then on the very invocation of the Khyber Pass became synonymous with subsequent Anglo-Afghan wars. It was the British intention to control Afghanistan in the face of a growing Russian threat.

Russia had indeed gotten the better of the Game by the end of World War I. It marked the beginning of England's decline as a player in the whole region. However, this development in no way forced Britain to abdicate her role completely. Britain still held on to the largest, disparate empire that ever existed, separated by seas and continents. London was not ready to relinquish this so quickly. After the end of World War I, Britain had established control over vast stretches of territory in the Middle East proper: She was in control of Mesopotamia, India, and regions in Asia and Africa. Britain projected a certain influence on Turkey, Iran, and Afghanistan, but for obvious reasons could not control these countries. For instance, when Amanullah Khan became king of Afghanistan, he became the first Third World ruler who dared recognize Soviet Russia under the very noses of the British. The latter, no matter how much they tried, could not prevent him from maintaining direct foreign ties. Concluding a treaty of friendship with the USSR in 1921, like his counterpart Reza Shah, Amanullah set out to modernize his country along secular lines.

Unfortunately for Amanullah, his grandiose schemes backfired. Neither as despotic as the Iranian shah, nor as unbending as the far-sighted Kemal Ataturk of Turkey, Amanullah's anticlericalism proved his undoing and brought him down in 1929 as the result of a Pushtun uprising that was not without instigation and support from British India. There were many in Afghanistan who felt that since Ottoman Turkey had ceased to exist, since Iran was also departing from its Moslem values under the Pahlavi dynasty, it was up to the Afghan government to set itself up as the heir to the Moslem caliphate. The feeble central authorities in Kabul perceived themselves to be within an imaginary safety net of the Soviet Union. Early in May 1921 Lenin could write to Amanullah conveying his "sympathy and confidence that no one will encroach on the independence of the High Afghan State either by force or by cunning."[2]

THE SLOW PENETRATION OF AFGHANISTAN BY THE SOVIET UNION

Possibly to conciliate the USSR, Afghanistan did not join the League of Nations until the Soviets did in the early 1930s. Later, in order not to antagonize the Soviets, Kabul joined neither the Baghdad Pact nor the CENTO "Northern Tier" Alliance aimed at the USSR. Kabul consistently remained neutral and nonaligned, while Pakistan and Iran became the linchpins in this Western alliance from 1954 onward.

It was on January 20, 1955, that Afghanistan established formal diplomatic relations with China. But in China's conflict with India, Afghanistan showed more sympathy for India; China was Pakistan's ally, and there was a lingering dispute between Pakistan and Afghanistan over "Pushtunistan." From the very outset, the Soviets had decided to support the Afghans' claims for a greater Pushtunistan, which also included the incorporation of Pakistan's province of Baluchistan into Afghanistan. Moscow reasoned thus: A Soviet-dominated Baluchistan in Pakistan is a strategic asset; it sits astride the entrance to the Persian Gulf, which is a strategic waterway for a nation that has no warm-water ports. Since Pakistan began closing its borders to Afghan transit, Afghanistan's land-locked economy became increasingly dependent on the USSR and on Iran for an outlet in its foreign trade. And since Afghanistan was at loggerheads with Iran over boundaries and water rights in the southwest, the Soviet Union became Afghanistan's major partner.

The Soviet game plan involved a slow but steady penetration of Afghanistan's economy. Prime Minister Mohammed Daoud received the lion's share of economic assistance from Moscow, everything from mining development and irrigation projects to oil exploration. The Soviets built the Salang Tunnel through the Hindu Kush to link Kabul by road to the USSR, and they designed and built the Bagram Airport in the capital. By 1973, Afghanistan had fallen completely within the Soviet sphere of influence. When in that year Daoud seized power from his cousin, King Zahir Shah, the coup was successful only because it was planned and organized by the Parchamite wing of the Marxist People's Democratic wing of the Democratic Party of Afghanistan (PDPA), which had been consistently pro-Soviet. The Parcham leaders in the past had held four government ministries.

Then, in the mid-1970s, Daoud (by then, the new king of Afghanistan) came increasingly under the sway of the shah of Iran, who was eager to expand his power across the entire region. The shah was soon offering him even more aid than was the USSR in areas such as railway construction, water sharing, and mining. The Afghan king accepted, but in return for the favor he unwisely allowed the Iranian Savak, the shah's secret police, to infiltrate the country. He believed that a secret police would, as in Iran, stamp out both religious conservatism and Marxism. He even proceeded to arrest the leaders of the Khalq and Parcham wings of the Communist Party; and it is this development that triggered the coup of April 1978 that brought the Marxists to power. As one of the more insightful analysts of the region pointedly observed, "Put in perspective, the 1978 Afghan coup emerges as one of the more disastrous legacies of the Shah's ambitious effort to roll back Soviet influence in the surrounding countries and to create a modern version of the ancient Persian empire."[3]

When the Soviets finally arrived in Afghanistan in December 1979, to shore up a weak and tottering regime, it was mainly in response to China, Pakistan, and Iran (not to mention the United States), which had been rendering material support to the tribal insurgents.[4] The decision to invade was taken by an inner group of four or five Politburo members, including Brezhnev and the defense minister, Dmitri Ustinov, over the heads of the KGB and against the better advice of Moscow's prestigious Institute of Economics of the World Socialist System.[5] The institute's memorandum, dated January 20, 1980, predicted the Soviet Union would face the combined opposition of the United States, NATO, China, and Moslem world, whose support it actually needs, not to mention "the rebel army of the Afghan feudal clerical circles."[6] The USSR thus had only itself to blame for damaging its standing both in the nonaligned movement and in the Islamic world. The victory of Moslem fundamentalism in Iran in February 1979 and the overthrow of the shah had given a powerful boost to Moslem fundamentalism in Afghanistan. Iran's Khomeini repeatedly denounced the new Marxist regime, grudgingly accepting many Afghan refugees, but allowing Pakistan to absorb the majority of roughly six million.

There is a certain logic in the proverbial saying "Nature abhors a vacuum." Afghanistan was like a ripe plum falling into the Kremlin's lap. There was really no one to lead the country, save a spineless administration and an effete leadership. Isolated from Western modernizing influences, coupled with sparse well-watered land, the Afghans lived in abject poverty before the communist takeover. The country had the highest infant mortality rate in the world, a third to a half of all infants dying in childhood. For anyone surviving childhood, life expectancy was about fifty years. Only 10 percent of the population was literate, and most of the big landowners were always absent from their lands, living either in Europe or the United States. The least one can say for the Afghan communists is that they tried to set up village schools and health care centers; but the wretched people wanted no part of it, and the Afghan resistance quickly turned against them.

Prior to and immediately after the Soviet invasion, Moscow was extremely upset over the feuds and quarrels inside the communist Khalq-Parcham coalition. Members of Parcham, whose members tended to be more conspiratorial, were recruited from among the Dari speakers of Kabul, mainly among university intellectuals. The Khalq "masses", under Mohammad Nur Taraki and Hafizullah Amin, were chiefly Pushtun, from the tribes in eastern and southern Afghanistan. Both factions tried to move too fast: Almost overnight they blindly disrupted time-honored social and economic relations; the Afghan communists would move from village to village expropriating lands and alienating the rural population in their headstrong attempts at land reform. If that were not enough, feuds soon degenerated into an outright physical elimination of each other. Amin actually killed Taraki in a palace shoot-out, before the Soviet army stepped in to maintain a semblance of order.

It would be naive to assume that the Soviets moved into Afghanistan and were motivated to do so by ideological considerations. That alone would simply not have been in keeping with *Realpolitik*'s balance-of-power game. On the other hand, we must also not discount the likelihood that the invasion and occupation of Afghanistan removed a threat to the Soviet Union's southern borders by preventing the installation of a Khomeini-type regime in Kabul. The fact that there was a successful communist coup in Afghanistan was definitely an ideological asset to the Kremlin leadership: It showed that progressive forces had taken over in a backward country. The fact that the Soviet military had to support it in the end was somewhat of a mixed blessing, since it actively involved the USSR in a region that was contiguous and strategically sensitive. Besides, something else—especially for the Red Army—proved to be just as important to the Soviet overall game plan in Southwest Asia: Afghanistan was to become a testing area for Soviet weaponry. This was indeed a cynical way of explaining Soviet actions. But then, the Russians had always been Machiavellian players.

While it cost the Soviet government one million roubles a day—1.7 million dollars at the then official exchange rate—consider the following factors in the Soviets' favor as long as they held on to Afghanistan. With the Soviet army well established on the southern borders of that country, the Soviet air force was only five hundred miles from the Strait of Hormuz. This was a very short striking distance from the Gulf Arab states. It out-flanked Iran from the east and was within reach of the U.S. fleet in the Indian Ocean, where a few Soviet warships and a single aircraft carrier plied the waters and barely kept pace with a vastly superior U.S. fleet there.[7] In the fighting in Afghanistan, the Soviet Union was able to test many new weapons: assault rifles; light and heavy military equipment; helicopter gun-ships; grenade launchers; self-propelled artillery; armored personnel car-riers; possible heat-repelling antidotes for the dreaded U.S.-made, heat-seeking, anti-aircraft stingers; battle management equipment, including the most advanced technology for command, control, and communications. The Soviets had not really had an opportunity to play such serious war games since 1945.

In Chapter 1 I discussed the value of the Wakhan Corridor for China's security in the discussion of the Pamir boundary settlement from which China had been excluded in 1895. When the Soviet army moved into Af-ghanistan, it occupied this three hundred kilometer long salient right up to the Kowtal-e Wakhjir Pass that opens onto the Chinese province of Xinjiang. There had never been an adequate road transportation in the corridor. As a result, Soviet aircraft, using makeshift landing strips, were forced to carry troops and military supplies into the area. Notwithstanding the difficulties posed by the terrain, the de facto possession of the Wakhan put the Soviet Union in a position to monitor, or even cut, if that proved necessary, the communication links between Pakistan and China. These communication links were between Gilgit and Xinjiang, making use of the Mintaka and Gardaneh-e Khunji passes through the Karakoram Mountains.

The Soviet occupation of the Wakhan Corridor was thus a very astute move. The Soviets had cut the only *direct* land route from China to the Afghan guerrillas. With the exception of a few, the local passes to both China and Pakistan were completely sealed, eliminating some, but not all, harassment from Afghan guerrillas in these border areas. Possession of the Wakhan gave the USSR a northern border with Pakistan, and it encouraged India to take a bolder stance against Pakistan in the former's age-old dispute over Kashmir, thereby increasing Pakistan's feelings of vulnerability. Al-though difficult terrain, the Wakhan was to prove useful as a supply and ordinance depot. To instill fear in the Chinese, nuclear missiles were at one point deployed near the passes. It came as no surprise when the People's Republic of China and the United States jointly decided to operate an electronic intelligence-gathering station in Xinjiang.[8] China's own early-warning system was simply obsolete against a preemptive Soviet strike.

From a geostrategic perspective, occupation of Afghanistan—by way of the Wakhan Corridor—tightened the encirclement of China.

THE END OF THE SOVIET OCCUPATION

Yet the invasion of Afghanistan hardly turned out to be advantageous to the Soviet Union, internally or externally. The war that ensued was not a popular one at home. Soviet Moslem soldiers defected. The Russians and Ukrainians felt out of place. From the start, the war was scantily reported in the Soviet media. In 1980, many Western countries followed the U.S. example of boycotting the Olympic Games held in Moscow. The general atmosphere of détente, so prevalent in the 1970s, was dead. The United States refused to ratify the SALT II accords that had been signed by Leonid Brezhnev and Jimmy Carter in Vienna in 1978. Ronald Reagan restricted the export of high-tech goods to the USSR, and the whole Afghan issue made it imperative that the United States push ahead with the Rapid Deployment Force, enhancing its naval presence in the Persian Gulf area, first under Carter and then, with greater vigor, under Reagan. All this played into the hands of the hawks in the Pentagon, who demanded an increased defense budget. Eventually the occupation became a great propaganda blow to Moscow. Further, in the early 1980s, it put a quick damper on a possible Soviet military intervention in Poland when that country was embroiled in a confrontation with the popular Solidarity movement. Meanwhile, as if it were not enough to be bogged down in the Afghan quagmire, the USSR was becoming increasingly alienated in the Third World and roundly condemned by the overwhelming majority of nonaligned states. The invasion was condemned, too, by the Arab League and at all the subsequent Islamic conferences.

Then, at long last, Kipling's Great Game moved one notch further to the Geneva UN-sponsored talks, where a deal on Afghanistan was finally hammered out on April 14, 1988, after six years of negotiations. The peace agreement, which was signed by the United States, the Soviet Union, Pakistan, and Afghanistan, consisted of four "instruments" and a memorandum. The gist of it was that Pakistan and Afghanistan agreed to observe mutual "noninterference" and "nonintervention," which meant (1) and end to arms supplies to the guerrillas through Pakistan and (2) Soviet withdrawal from Afghanistan over a period of nine months. Both Pakistan and Afghanistan pledged to encourage the voluntary return of refugees to their homes. The USSR and the United States agreed to respect Afghanistan's neutrality and nonaligned status. The negotiations also provided for a small force of UN observers to be stationed in Afghanistan. Finally, there followed two private understandings that would complicate matters in the future. The United States and the Soviet Union agreed that either was free to aid its Afghan allies during the nine-month withdrawal if the other did. Another point of ambivalence was that Diego Cordovez, the UN mediator, together with the four parties to this agreement, was to open talks with a view to setting up a coalition government for all Afghans.

The idea of a coalition government for Afghanistan was initially a Soviet one. It was supported by many in the West and especially by the Indian leadership in New Delhi. The proposal for a coalition government also called for the return of the former king Zahir Shah to the throne in Afghanistan, setting up a system in which all sections of society would have a say in decision making, including the communists. But the idea of having Zahir Shah return to Kabul was predicated on having a temporary, transitional regime that would create a national consensus on a future government. Looked at objectively, it was not a bad idea. The king was supported by three of the more moderate parties in the rebel alliance, but he was violently opposed by the other four.

In any case, the whole proposition fell apart early in 1988, when India's minister of state for foreign affairs, Natwar Singh, visited the former monarch and made the contact public. The visit allowed opponents to brand Zahir Shah as the Indian candidate, and therefore his candidacy was a questionable proposition. It was unacceptable to Pakistan and to the fundamentalists in the Afghan alliance. It was also categorically rejected by the Shi'i leadership in Iran.

For their part, the Pakistanis, while extremely active in the UN peace talks, no less actively supported the formation of a *mujahedeen*-dominated interim government, an idea ultimately dropped when they realized how impracticable such a thing might be to organize on Pakistani soil. This, in any case, was Zia ul-Hak's own idea. Elections were to be held in Pakistan in November of 1988. So, it was simply better for Islamabad to support and encourage a UN-brokered peace and pretend to acquiesce in something as vague as a "coalition government," which, arguably, was just as impracticable in the long term. The question of a future government in Afghanistan was thus left dangerously open, with Zia ul-Hak and his generals secretly supporting the rebels and in the same breath signing the Geneva peace agreement. It was as if Islamabad were running with the rabbit and hunting with the hounds. But Pakistan later became increasingly bogged down in political inertia when the November 1988 elections brought Benazir Bhutto to power in Islamabad with a strong commitment to democracy and a neutral policy on Afghanistan. Pakistan's military authorities were fearful this would play right into the hands of the Soviets.

THE AFGHAN RESISTANCE: FREEDOM FIGHTERS OR REBEL BASMACHI?

Not surprisingly, the Geneva agreement on Soviet troop withdrawals from Afghanistan set the stage for even greater turmoil and potential instability in the region. This superpower agreement, supported by Pakistan and the Soviet-backed government of Afghanistan, was never regarded as a legitimate accord by the Afghan *mujahedeen*.

With the Soviet troop withdrawal, it was widely believed that the communist regime led by the newly installed president Najibullah had virtually no chance of surviving an anticipated onslaught by the *mujahedeen* guerrillas. The latter had, despite the pact, vowed to continue their *jihad*—or Islamic holy war. Gulbudin Hekmatyar, the most outspoken rebel leader, compared Najibullah's regime to a "ramshackle wall whose only studs are Soviet forces." "Once those studs are removed," he said, "the wall will collapse."[9] Hekmatyar's intent was the creation of a fundamentalist Islamic society and government, similar to Khomeini's Iran, though it was to be Sunni and backed by Pakistan's Zia ul-Hak, from whom Hekmatyar had been receiving the bulk of the material support.

There are interesting paradoxes in Hekmatyar's plans. It is Hekmatyar who was widely suspected of being more interested in taking power in Kabul himself than in getting rid of the Soviet-backed regime. Paradoxically, not all the rebels thought alike; the Pakistan-based resistance leaders and the commanders in the field have not always agreed. Let us take a closer look at some of these paradoxes in the resistance movement.

Assisted by mercenaries and foreign money and equipment, or Soviet defectors (who were themselves generally Moslems), these rebels have so far been led by a half-dozen, half-baked, volatile and frequently competitive rivals. They are Sunni fundamentalists whose only common bond is an abiding hatred of the Soviets and the Afghan communists. The main Afghan rebel group, Barhanudin Rabbani's Jamiat-i-Islami party, exists in an uneasy rivalry with Hekmatyar's Hizbe-i-Islami; these are challenged in turn by Younis Khalis's Hizbe-i-Islami Afghanistan and the National Islamic Front of Afghanistan, led by Pir Sayyed Ahmad Gailani, whose only claim to fame is that he is a hereditary Sufi saint. Then there is the more quixotic Ittehad-i-Islami, led by Rasul Sayyaf, a Wahhabi Moslem, who used to obtain enormous financial support from the Saudis. Last is the National Front for the Rescue of Afghanistan, led by Sigbatullah Mojadedi, a Westernized academic with monarchist leanings who hails from a prominent religious family. To be sure, in 1986 these groups had concluded a solemn alliance called the Islamic Unity of Afghan Mujahedeen, with a supreme council composed of the leaders of the principal parties. But this bogus unity only gave them some credibility—probably in justification of increased arms shipments from the United States. The various leaders have since been rotating their authority. When President Reagan received Rabbani in the summer of 1986, seeking badly needed anti-aircraft weapons (the shoulder-fired, heat-seeking stingers), his trip was called a public-relations disaster, while the other leaders in Peshawar were calling Rabbani unrepresentative of the movement.[10]

Considering the deeply rooted mutual grievances of the rival partisan groups, their temporary unity was always an illusory one, all the more so when they savored the forced withdrawal of a superpower's superior military forces. Hekmatyar's Khomeini-style radicalism contrasts with Rabbani's more moderate approach, a fact that in the past had resulted in battles and serious casualties between the feuding groups. On two occasions at least, Hekmatyar's forces, blocking the Andarab route in the winter skirmishes of 1983 and 1984, severed the supply lines to (Rabbani's) Jamiat's stronghold. It was estimated that over a five-year period at least six million Afghans had become refugees due to these internecine guerrilla actions. As the Soviets began departing from Afghanistan, Rabbani urged the guerrillas to refrain from harassing them, arguing that it would only slow down their withdrawal. To continue fighting would be tantamount to squandering valuable resources. But with the battle for Kabul in progress beginning in early August 1988, as Soviet and Afghan government forces withdrew from the outermost of the three defense rings around the city, the emotive Hekmatyar set about shelling the capital—firing no less than 170 rockets in a single week against a defenseless civilian population.

Even the most popular field commander, Ahmad Shah Massoud, a member of Rabbani's faction, agreed to stop attacking the departing troops. Temporarily, the competing guerrilla groups did accede, under Pakistani pressure, to a coalition government in Kabul. However, they deliberately sabotaged it by choosing a nonentity, who lacked any broad support, to lead the coalition. Their Machiavellian tactics resembled the broad tradition of Afghan politics, very similar, in a comic sense, to the communist Parcham and Khalq factions that have been fighting each other since 1965.

At the same time, Iran was deliberately sending mixed signals over Afghanistan. Expressing its Shi'i Islam, Iran has been showing a marked hostility to Afghani fundamentalism, which is expressed in a Sunni tradition. Only 20 percent of the Afghans are Shi'i Moslems, and they are not the dominant Pushtuns, the majority Afghan ethnic group. Nor does there appear to be any Shi'i Moslem leader of comparable stature in the whole resistance movement. Similarly, there is evidence to suggest that the Afghans in Iran, who have fled there primarily as refugees, are treated as third-class citizens.

On the other hand, the potential is there for a convenient rapprochement between Iran and the Soviet Union.[11] A beleaguered Iran, confronted by U.S. military might in the Persian Gulf, having fought a losing war of attrition with Iraq, seeing the fortunes of Iraq fade in a conflict with a U.S.-led multinational force in the Gulf, could very well give serious consideration to Soviet policy initiatives. What does this mean? While in late 1987 Teheran forcefully rejected a Soviet proposal to return deposed Zahir Shah to the Afghan throne, at least as the titular head of a coalition, it appears that the Iranians will now be dependent on Soviet military hardware. The Iranians might even be expected to acquiesce in any plans Moscow may have for a future government in Kabul.

Many believed that Kabul, the Afghan capital, would fall like the proverbial house of cards as soon as Soviet troops were completely withdrawn. This did not happen. But since the withdrawal, evacuation permits allowing entry to the Soviet Union to top Afghan communists are said to have been issued. Speculation has been rife that mass Afghan army desertions would parallel the Soviet withdrawal, with some Afghan army commanders intimating their intention to surrender to the resistance to avoid further bloodshed. A rumor also circulated saying that the celebrated "Lion of the Panjshir," Commander Ahmad Shah Massoud, operating in northeastern Afghanistan, had already concluded a nonaggression pact with the Soviets.[12] But Massoud gave the lie to these reports, arguing that it was President Najibullah who tried to coax him into a coalition, offering him a choice of top government posts in exchange for peace. It is said that Massoud has vowed to fight on and is waiting for a final showdown with government forces in Kabul.[13]

If that comes to pass, Western analysts and observers, and, for that matter, their Soviet counterparts, would be faced with a series of interrelated questions that have to be answered prior to the formulation of any potential policy for so unstable a region. For example, how long is President Najibullah supposed to hold on to Kabul, and, for that matter, does it really matter? There was speculation at the time of the withdrawal that the Soviet ambassador, Yuli Vorontsov, was trying to persuade the Communist Party's factions to settle their differences and start talking to the rebels about sharing power. How long could Kabul possibly survive if it were to lose access to the Salang Tunnel, which cuts through the Hindu Kush, connecting Kabul to Mazar-i-Sharif and ultimately to the Soviet Union? Surely Najibullah realizes that without logistical support and resupply, he could not hold on to the Afghan capital indefinitely.

In the interim, this scenario has not come to pass. On the contrary, fortifications are going up around Kabul. The Soviet army has continued with the delivery of arms, and they are currently reinforcing the military infrastructure, as well as placing additional artillery, minefields, missiles, armor, and artillery inside and around the Kabul garrison. It appears that the Soviets are buying time. By holding on to Kabul, the capital, for at least a year or two longer, maintaining the Jalalabad stronghold near the eastern, Pakistani frontier, holding fast to Kandahar in the south and to Herat near the Iranian border, the rebel leaders may be compelled to come to the negotiating table and form a power-sharing government yet. If that were to come to pass, the Soviets would be in a better position to formulate a new Soviet-Afghan border strategy.

After leaving Afghanistan, the Soviets left in place a well-trained, seasoned army of Afghan regulars. The Kabul regime has airpower, whereas the resistance forces do not and will probably never have it. Doubtless, Western media reports exaggerated the number of defections from the regular Afghan forces—to make it appear that the rebels were superior warriors and were morally right in fighting the communists.[14] In point of fact, in the spring of 1989 the guerrillas launched three successive attacks against the Jalalabad fortress, not too far from the Khyber Pass. Prodded into this dastardly act of launching major offensives by Pakistan's military intelligence (ISI), the guerrillas faced an outcome that turned into a major disaster. As many as three thousand of the rebels lost their lives, and a large quantity of U.S.-made weapons was seized. The ISI had long been supporting Hekmatyar as well; the Pakistani military had been giving him the largest share of the arms provided by the United States and Saudi Arabia.[15]

Hekmatyar launched a major offensive on October 12, 1990, taking advantage of the dry ground before the winter snows made campaigning very difficult. The other rebel leaders refused to join him, and Hekmatyar's men were cut to pieces by the regular army's armed sorties and rocket attacks. The only time the rebels did well against a government garrison was during the Battle of Khost, which they captured in the spring of 1991, without the assistance of Hekmatyar. The Khost garrison simply surrendered without much fighting, probably double-crossed by mercenary tribal warriors who changed sides when the siege was becoming too much for them. Hekmatyar would have shot all the government troops when they surrendered. But Commander Jalaludin Haqqani offered the garrison of Khost an amnesty, which was honored.

The opposition to Hekmatyar has a large following. Among them, the famous field commander Ahmad Shah Massoud was reported to have gone to Pakistan from his Panjshir Valley stronghold for the first time in eleven years to help organize an anti-Hekmatyar coalition. There he met the political leader of the alliance of Pakistan-based *mujahedeen* parties, Sibghatullah Mojadidi. What is disquieting to them all—especially to Hekmatyar—is Teheran's obvious tilt toward Moscow and the U.S. Congress's plan to cut aid to the rebels by one-third (the total was approximately 200 million dollars in 1991). The American president could suddenly stop aid to the resistance altogether by 1992. The Saudis are angry because Hekmatyar mindlessly supported Saddam Hussein in the Gulf War against the U.S.-led coalition while some rebel volunteers came to fight for the Allies. Moreover, U.S. and Soviet diplomats are moving closer to a Cambodia-style peace solution for Afghanistan, an arrangement providing for some power sharing between Najibullah and the rebel parties until an election could be held. But the guerrillas have stated that they would never deal with President Najibullah; and so the war in Afghanistan will continue, no matter what policy changes the Gorbachev reforms bring in the Soviet Union.

It is inconceivable that the Soviets, the alleged masters of the ability to think three moves ahead, would withdraw from Afghanistan without creating conditions that would maximize their potential future policy options. Besides, the decision to invade Afghanistan, although denounced by Gorbachev's leadership as a crime,[16] was made and carried out by a latter-day Politburo, together with the Red Army chief-of-staff. Officered in the main by ethnic Russian soldiers, that army—Red or just Russian—is the least likely to be moved by the liberal, market-oriented reforms in the USSR and will resist most of them. A right-wing coup, orchestrated by the armed forces, cannot be ruled out in the Soviet Union, now or in the near future, in view of the anarchy and the near collapse of the Soviet economy. This brings me to the next point: What action ought to be taken to stave off threats to the Soviet Moslem republics in the event of an ultimate fundamentalist *mujahedeen* victory in Afghanistan? And, in these times of uncertainty in the Soviet Union, by whom?

FUTURE PROSPECTS FOR THE SOVIETS

Afghanistan has been referred to as the Soviet Vietnam, and the circumstances, in the broadest parameters, do indeed resemble the U.S. Vietnamese quagmire. The Soviet problem, as was the Americans' in Vietnam, has been one of fighting a determined adversary of true believers. While Vietnamese nationalism was based on a burning desire to reject a series of Japanese, French, and U.S. occupiers, that of Afghanistan is founded on Islamic fundamentalism.

This fundamentalist nationalism, coupled with the almost insurmountable logistical and manpower requirements necessary to subdue a dedicated force of *mujahedeen*, in the face of internal Soviet demands for reform, literally overwhelmed the superior Soviet military forces. The Soviet face-saving withdrawal, motivated by a desire not unlike that of the Americans in Vietnam to cut substantial losses in a no-win situation, raises several interesting questions as to Afghanistan's future territorial integrity.

In the protracted Afghan war, the Soviets experienced particular difficulty in containing the *mujahedeen* in territories adjacent to the Pakistan border, being forced to concede several areas to the rebels while concentrating their efforts on controlling major urban areas, particularly Kabul. One can now imagine the Kremlin leadership, in conjunction with the Soviet general staff, developing contingency plans for successive defense lines. Having conceded southern border areas to the rebels, Kabul becomes the second line of defense—provided that it can be held for an appreciable length of time. Should it fall to the rebels, the Soviets will be faced with a number of virtually unpalatable choices. Should they evacuate the communist regime, granting it sanctuary elsewhere, as the Americans did with Chiang Kai-shek on Formosa in 1949 or with some of their supporters after the

fall of Saigon in 1975? Conversely, in a face-saving gesture to their friends
and newfound allies (primarily the capitalist Europeans) in other parts of
the world, would the Soviet Union be prepared to resettle several hundred
thousand supporters of the communist regime in refugee camps in the
USSR? Recognizing that this latter alternative is not acceptable, the Soviet-
backed defense line may be moved to the north of Hindu Kush, reestab-
lishing the Afghan Communist Party, and whoever the future leader of that
government might be, in Mazar-i-Sharif, the capital of northern Afghanistan.
Needless to say, the Soviets still possess a considerable number of assets.
Whatever else happens internally in the Soviet Union, let us consider the
following advantages and trump cards that are still in Moscow's hand.

THE AFGHAN SECRET POLICE

Even if the Parcham-Khalq regime's forces prove to be very weak, plagued
by desertions, militarily effective only behind fortifications, the present
Kabul government will have the dreaded WAD (Afghan Secret Service)
(formerly KHAD, former State Information Service of Afghanistan) as an
instrument of control and terror long after the Soviet withdrawal. Westerners rarely hear of this organization; what is it, and what will be its
importance in postwithdrawal Afghanistan?

KHAD, the acronym for Khalidamate Aetilaati Daulati (State Information
Service), has had between twenty-five and thirty thousand agents, em-
ployees, and informers. It is patterned after, and organized by, the Soviet
KGB. President Najibullah, KHAD's former head, granted it enhanced status
when he replaced Babrak Karmal as the Communist Party leader. Najibullah
made it the Ministry of Internal Security, an instrument of coercion, terror,
and espionage. While theoretically accountable to the Afghan Politburo,
KHAD is virtually controlled by KGB liaison officers operating under diplomatic cover at the Soviet embassy in Kabul. It will probably continue to
do so even in the unlikely event that there will be no Soviet embassy at
Kabul.

While WAD was under tight Soviet control, with at least fifty-seven Soviet
advisors attached to each directorate, its indigenous Afghani leaders were
Parchamite communists, who used WAD to suppress their Khalq rivals.
Evidence suggests that through interrogations, tortures, and assassinations,
WAD had conducted a reign of terror against the Afghan resistance. However, its main contribution to regional instability was clandestine activity
directed against Pakistan. Through infiltration of refugee camps near Peshawar in Pakistan, WAD not only encouraged the Pushtun and the Baluchis
to oppose General Zia ul-Haq's military administration but also fostered
hostility by local Pakistani communities toward the refugees. There is little
doubt now that this espionage and intelligence service, believing that a
Pakistani arms dump at Islamabad and Rawalpindi held supplies destined

for the Afghan guerrillas, was behind demolition of the dump. That act killed ninety-four and injured more than one thousand in late April 1988. Similarly, the blame for the assassination in Peshawar of at least thirty-seven guerrilla commanders in the period from the war's beginning to January 1991 was laid squarely at the feet of KHAD. In addition, WAD conducted an ingenious misinformation campaign; its actions, such as forging Hekmatyar's orders of the day, caused partisan leaders to admit they were often its unwitting agents.

But the greatest coup to date brought off by this secret police was when, on August 17, 1988, Pakistan's President Zia ul-Haq was killed in a mysterious explosion shortly after his aircraft took off from a remote airport near the Indian border. With him perished General Akhtar Abdul Rehman, chairman of the joint chiefs-of-staff committee along with U.S. ambassador Arnold Raphel and Herbert Wassom, chief U.S. defense representative to Pakistan. The assassination of the Pakistani leader was most likely planned for weeks, if not months. If Najibullah had planned the assassination, he must have foreseen it as a blow to the Afghan resistance, particularly to Hekmatyar, Zia's protégé. It is unlikely, however, that the WAD would have also wanted to eliminate the Americans, which was probably an unavoidable accident. But the CIA continued funneling arms to the Afghan rebels while Soviet troops were pulling out, and the fighting around Kabul had been very intense. It was therefore the perfect time to dispose of Zia ul-Haq. It must be pointed out that the only other enemies the Pakistani leader had would come from the internal opposition led by Benazir Bhutto or perhaps the Indian government. But neither of these could possibly be regarded as maliciously efficient to pull off anything nearly as spectacular as the Afghan WAD.

Why? The reason is self-explanatory. Zia had simply wanted his own fundamentalists in Kabul, even at the expense of the moderate factions among the guerrillas, and this fact was leading to increased tension not only within the Afghan ranks but within the United Nations, which was becoming more and more irritated with Pakistan's blatant breaches of the Geneva agreement. One of these violations was Pakistan's sudden involvement in the fighting: Pakistani officers would go into Afghanistan to direct operations, or to supervise the use of missiles and stingers against Afghan and Soviet aircraft. The Pakistanis often penalized the local commanders who did not fall in with their plans. A rift was beginning to appear between the commanders in the field and the Pakistani-supported rebel leaders. None of this was lost on the Soviet authorities who were still in control in Afghanistan. The Soviets must have seen Zia as the leading obstacle to a dignified and speedy retreat of their forces from the war-torn land. In this sense, the surgical strike was in every way reminiscent of the Israeli Mossad's assassination of Abu Jihad, a Palestinian terrorist mastermind, in Tunis just a few months before.

The divide-and-conquer scenario described above is supported by a number of factors—mainly geographic and ethnic. Afghanistan is divided naturally into north and south by the Hindu Kush, the formidable mountain range cutting across the country from the Wakhan Corridor near China to the north of Herat near the Iranian frontier. The Hindu Kush is more than a geographical demarcation; it is, perhaps more importantly, a very significant ethnic dividing line. In Afghanistan's ethnic and tribal potpourri, the Pushtuns are concentrated in the area south of the Hindu Kush, adjacent to the Northwest Frontier Province, where their Pakistani ethnic-tribal cousins live. Further to the south, the Afghan Baluchis straddle a common frontier with their respective Pakistani cousins. However, north of the Hindu Kush, which is contiguous to the Central Asian Soviet republics (Turkmen, Uzbek, and Tajik), one finds ethnic groups of Turkic descent, Uzbeks and Turkmens, or Tajiks and Hazaras, who speak an Iranian dialect.

As already indicated, all Afghans tend to see the world primarily in the context of ethnic and tribal loyalties; they have never been united, except in the face of a common enemy, and even this unity, as the war has demonstrated, has been short-lived. Moreover, if the Afghans were in fact left to themselves, their nation, like the Arab, still remains to be created. Considering that one of the motives of the 1979 Soviet invasion was to preempt the contagion of the Soviet Central Asian republics by Islamic fundamentalism, it is unlikely that the Soviets would overlook the dangers inherent in an Islamic fundamentalist regime in Kabul. The Soviets' intent may very well be to establish Najibullah, or another puppet, in Mazar-i-Sharif, thereby establishing a buffer zone just below their southern borders.

South Afghanistan would not be without precedence: Consider the partition of Ireland, Germany, Korea, Yemen, and Vietnam. The Soviet experience with Azerbaijan could be viewed as a model for their potential diplomatic behavior. Having occupied Iranian Azerbaijan in 1941, the Soviets established a communist regime and attempted to maintain it until forced to withdraw in 1946, after immense international pressure. Accordingly, there is a Soviet Azerbaijan, whose population is Shi'i (Azeri), and an Iranian Azerbaijan, whose citizens are likewise Azeri-speaking Shi'ites. However, in view of the great Soviet recalcitrance to withdraw in 1946, it may be unrealistic to expect the Soviets to be less reluctant to permit settlement, populated by people of similar ethnic origin, in areas contiguous to their Central Asian borders.

The Soviet planners, or Russian planners as the case might be, may be rationalizing some form of partition as their fallback position, hence accomplishing several goals in both domestic and international politics. By retaining the north, they would have a tangible to show for their heavy loss of human life, estimated to be in the range of fifteen thousand killed, and an unspecified number of wounded. At the same time, the Soviets would send an international signal that the Brezhnev Doctrine[17] is at least alive—if not all that well. Finally, the Soviets could perceive their action as establishing a buffer around their southern borders, a move of crucial importance should South Afghanistan succumb to Islamic fundamentalism. This move could serve as an ideological justification, not only for Soviet citizens, but also for an exasperated political leadership, and that is what the withdrawal represents, after a brutal nine-year war. Nations or communities who are ethnically and linguistically kin and living on both sides of a frontier, will always be drawn to each other culturally. This is certainly true, by way of analogy, of the Christian Armenians and the Moslem Kurds, both of whom have yet to achieve statehood and whose populations live among other nations. Tajiks and Uzbeks are cases in point in Afghanistan, and this ought to be a trump card in the Soviets' favor. Should the partition of Afghanistan take place, what are the implications for the West and for the stability in the region?

If the Afghan communists transfer their headquarters to Mazar-i-Sharif, behind the natural barrier of the Hindu Kush, the various ethnic groups could engage in a war to liberate their homelands. The question arises as to whether the Pushtuns will pursue their struggle to the north of the Hindu Kush and whether the Turkic groups can muster sufficient force to match the Soviet and Afghan forces, particularly since the latter would be operating in a more hospitable area, with greater access to Soviet supplies. At the same time, one must take into consideration that the northern Afghan provinces and the Soviet southern republics have been of late signing several important trade and commercial deals.[18] Finally, the *mujahedeen* will lose the benefits of their proximity to the Pakistani border.

The West has used Pakistani territory for logistical supply and support to the *mujahedeen*. Should the rebels liberate Kabul, it, along with other major towns, could become a target for the Afghan communists, who would then contend the existence of an international war between sovereign countries. Any Western attempt at supplying arms to a *mujahedeen* regime in Kabul might elicit a Soviet accusation that the West was reneging on the Geneva agreement. The Soviets had, after all, insisted on a nonaligned, neutral Afghanistan as a condition of their withdrawal. Similarly, any attempt by the West to supply the *mujahedeen* would give the Najibullah regime in Mazar-i-Sharif a legal pretext to invite the Soviets back in.

The future might show a partition line drawn from Kushka in the Turkmen Soviet Socialist Republic, past Bala Murghab in northwestern Afghanistan, following the Murghab River and the Hindu Kush, leading to, and including, the Wakhan Corridor. Najibullah and his supporters might find pitching their tents behind this line to be preferable to incarceration in Uzbekistan's refugee camps.

Should the above analysis prove correct, even as a long-term prognostication, it does not explain adequately what might be in store for Afghanistan and the rival tribes in the rest of the country as they win the entire territory back from the central government. Only one thing is certain: With hegemony in the north, the Soviets will be in a position to either grant or withhold support at will to competing groups. The Soviets may view this as preferable to mediation between feuding factions of the Afghan Communist Party, which was the reason why they invaded Afghanistan in the first place.

One must exhibit more than a passing degree of sympathy for the tasks faced by the rebels after the Soviet withdrawal. Whether the rebels are present-day Basmachi or not becomes irrelevant. With the exception of Hekmatyar, they are certainly not brigands or bandits. The worst one could say is that they appear to behave and fight like an unruly mob in need of a compassionate and mature leader. If they do carry the day, take Kabul and Jalalabad, it is almost a foregone conclusion that there will be a breakdown in social order, with attendant anarchy and massacres as old scores are settled. The reestablishment of a strong central government, given the past history of this land, appears to be problematic, if not impossible, in both the short and medium terms. Also, if Hekmatyar is eliminated, there will be endless bickering among the resistance field commanders as they attempt to consolidate their positions. From this action may emerge a patchwork of self-rule areas, a Balkanization of Afghanistan, which could reduce ultimately the Pushtun monopoly on power. Again, Iran may, now that its war with Iraq is over, come to the assistance of a Shi'i minority such as the Hazaras.

To many, the idea of a Balkanization of Afghanistan may appear too unorthodox an analysis, too removed from reality. Any analysis depends, however, on how one reads an ever evolving reality. There have been many changes in Afghanistan. The ethnic makeup of the country has changed drastically. For instance, the proportion of Pushtuns has decreased from 39 percent to 22 percent. One of the few U.S. observers who believes in the "Balkanization" thesis, Stephen Blank, reports that the Tajiks now constitute the largest group, with 34 percent of the population.[19] He, too, makes a case for a separate identity in northern Afghanistan, culturally, administratively, militarily, and economically. Blank concludes that there is "an enormous and constant interpenetration of Afghanistan by Soviet Central Asian cadres and professionals whose purpose is clearly to cement ties of ethnic affiliation with Soviet Moslems."[20] Yet many will surely say that this is an unlikely scenario in view of the current nationalities problems in Soviet Central Asia and the general breakdown of the Soviet system and its Moslem populations. Indeed, the USSR is experiencing a widescale disintegration, even among the Soviet Moslems. But I will come back to this question in Chapter 5, when I deal with Soviet Islam.

Thus the ten-year Afghan war, with its horrendous casualties, has scarred completely what is essentially a primitive society. With an estimated one million Afghans killed, the direct loss of human life exceeds the losses in all the Arab-Israeli conflicts, the Algerian War of Independence, and the Iran-Iraq war. Casualities are almost equal to all the post-1945 Indo-China wars, including the U.S. war in Vietnam. The plight of the survivors is only marginally better: six million languishing in refugee camps and three million without homes. Altogether, the dead, the fled, and the dislocated amount to half the prewar population of fifteen million! For two centuries, foreign armies marched and countermarched on Afghan soil in a game of power politics that gave the foreigners absolutely nothing. What is worse, the Afghans will now be more dependent upon these foreigners than ever before. This is a tragic comment indeed on a state that has as yet to constitute itself. However, statehood and the rivalry of foreign powers is no longer an issue, because that cannot be helped. What matters now is that Afghans are in dire need of humanitarian aid for the almost insurmountable tasks of refugee resettlement, rural reconstruction, and the establishment of political stability. But if the competing factions never find a modicum of common ground that can lead to some semblance of unity, the war will continue in Afghanistan and so will the constant game to influence it.

NOTES

1. Russian envoys lost their lives in a similar fashion. The great tsarist playwright Griboedov was likewise "hacked to pieces," outside his door in Teheran.

2. V. I. Lenin, *Sobranie Sochinienii* (Collected Works) (Moscow: Politizdat, 1971).

3. Selig Harrison, "The Shah, Not Kremlin, Touched Off Afghan Coup," *Washington Post*, May 13, 1979.

4. The best account of this is in Henry Bradsher, *The Soviet Union and Afghanistan* (Durham, N.C.: Duke University Press, 1983).

5. See *Novaia Zemlya* (New Land) (Moscow: Nauka, 1986), 33.

6. Ibid.

7. This information is the author's own, culled from a trip to southern Iran and Pakistan in June of 1981. Of course, the U.S. fleet in the Persian Gulf is far greater today in the wake of the turmoil over Iraq's attack on Kuwait. The Soviet fleet was never larger than the figures I have given. See also Anthony Cordesman, *The Persian Gulf and the West* (Boulder, Colo.: Westview Press, 1987). Also see my chapter on Iran in the present book for more details.

8. *New York Times*, March 3, 1984.

9. Miron Rezun, "Afghanistan's Twists," *International Perspectives* 7, no. 3 (March 1989).

10. Zalmay Khalilzad, "The War in Afghanistan," *International Journal*, vol. 4, no. 2 (1986), 6.

11. See the chapter on Iran.

12. *Economist*, October 22, 1988, p. 44.

13. See the story on the Lion of the Panjshir in *Time*, October 31, 1988.

14. A number of books appeared on Afghanistan in the 1980s. The best collection

of fables and inaccuracies is contained in Roxanna Klass's *Afghanistan: The Great Game Revisited* (New York: United States Information Agency, 1987).

15. *Economist*, October 20, 1990.

16. *Pravda*, October 10, 1989.

17. Moscow might even call it by another, less irritating name. The Brezhnev Doctrine could even be reactivated by a right-wing Russian regime. It states that any interference in Moscow's sphere of influence will be met with armed retaliation.

18. *Kazakhstanskaia Pravda* (Alma-Ata), June 13, 1990.

19. See Stephen Blank, " 'Glasnost' and Afghanistan," in *Glasnost, Perestroika and the Socialist Community*, ed. Charles Bukowski and J. Richard Walsh. (New York: Praeger, 1990), 120.

20. Ibid., 122.

4

Iran in the Mist

Writing this section on Iran is indeed an overwhelming task. The only consistency about this nation is its inconsistency. Much of the analysis of Iran's behavior requires a careful evaluation of its relationship with the Arabs, especially with Iraq. In that relationship, the superpowers are equally important, especially the United States. Until Saddam Hussein's invasion of Kuwait, in past publications I described Iran's conduct as that of a "pariah" in the region. It is no longer that; things have changed with such breathtaking swiftness that it becomes exceedingly onerous to evaluate the position of this country, given the unprecedented change of circumstances in the space of a single year.

Suffice it to say that I was not surprised that Saddam Hussein would one day try to invade and annex Kuwait, that he would covet the whole of the Gulf region, that his designs were first typically Iraqi, and secondly pan-Arabic. In this region of the world, the bulk of the Arab people, devout Moslems, nonbelievers, Arab Christians, the poor and disadvantaged, some Arab leaders (although they do not—or dare not—admit it) regarded him, when he reached the pinnacle of his power, as something of a Nasser or Saladin.[1] There is but one exception—the Iranians. The Iranians might have won the war against Iraq and, after the passing of Khomeini, would probably no longer have posed a threat to Southwest Asia and the Middle East had it not been for the blatant interference of the United States. By supporting Iraq, Washington inadvertently had strengthened Baghdad's hand in this game of territorial expansion, indirectly contributing to tipping the balance in favor of Saddam Hussein. This encouraged Saddam in his designs for

Iraqi domination. I am certainly not alone in making this contention; my purpose is to establish this as a fact beyond any doubt.

The post-Khomeini period will become critical to our understanding of how this Great Game will continue without Khomeini. For until his death the Islamic Republic of Iran was not really given serious consideration by the United States. At the height of the Salman Rushdie affair, even Britain, and the rest of Western Europe too, was not quite able or willing to understand what was taking place in Iran's domestic affairs. Why has Iran so often been maligned, misunderstood, rejected, and condemned? No doubt, the Americans themselves will one day admit that they backed the wrong horse by siding with Saddam Hussein, now that they realize that in Khomeini, a visionary ecclesiastic—some say a "mad" and "irrational" one—there is genuinely little to compare with the demonic perfidy of the Iraqi dictator.

IMPERIAL IRAN'S RELATIONS WITH ARABS AND JEWS

The land of Zoroaster had been conquered by the Arab Moslems in the seventh century. When the Pahlavi monarchy was established, the leading intellectuals of Iran were keenly mindful of the nation's pre-Islamic past. "Pahlavism" made official a national mythology that began as far back as the nineteenth century, under a weak Qajar rule. It was a vigorous nationalism aimed at glorifying the pre-Islamic past and Iranian kingship dating from the fifth century B.C. The high point was reached at Persepolis in 1971 under the second Pahlavi king, Mohammad Reza, in the celebration of twenty-five hundred years of monarchy. What this all meant was that although the Iranians remained Moslems, the idea of Islamic ideology was discarded from the moment Reza Shah, the first Pahlavi monarch, ascended the Persian throne in 1925.[2]

The architect of this secular, nationalist society was not really Reza Shah, however.[3] Rather, it was a man who helped put him on the throne and conducted the diplomacy of the nation by himself—Reza's minister of the court, Teymourtash.[4] Teymourtash and the governing triumvirate he headed had Iranian history rewritten to such a point that it played down the whole Islamic period. The articulate, Westernized segments of the population were quick to appreciate this. Before long, a nationalist campaign was promoted to galvanize the support of the Iranian people beyond the intellectual strata by extolling the virtues of an ancient Aryan civilization in symbols like *Iran-e-Bastan* (ancient Iran), and in the purity of the Persian language *Farsi ye ser'e* (pure Persian). These symbols set Iran apart from its immediate neighbors, both Arab and non-Arab, but more particularly the Arabs, whom Iranian leaders regarded as "barbarian" (*Vahshigari arab*, the uncouth Arab).

These invocations were one of the reasons behind a desire for expansionism and territorial aggrandizement. One notable incident took place at the time King Amnanullah of Afghanistan was deposed in 1929 on a surge of Moslem fundamentalism. Teymourtash in fact sent a whole army to the Afghan border in a bid to wrest the Afghan province of Herat in a moment of Afghan weakness.[5] Mutual accommodations between Iran and Afghanistan followed only after Soviet and Turkish mediation. But similar territorial claims were made in this period on Bahrain and on territories in the Persian Gulf perceived to be inhabited by Arabs of Persian stock. Claims to Soviet territory—particularly to Soviet Azerbaijan and parts of Central Asia—were also made both to the English and, especially, to the Nazis at a time when there was great sympathy in Iran for the German (Aryan) cause prior to and during World War II.[6]

However, it was not until the advent of Mohammad Reza Shah, Reza Shah's son, that Iran seriously began propagating its age-old national mythology and was able to arrogate to itself a preeminent role in the affairs of the Gulf. In the latter 1960s and during the 1970s, oil revenues had made Iran a second-ranking world power in international politics, the "gendarme" of Persian Gulf security. During this period it was considered on a par with such states as India, despite the fact that India supports a population twenty times as large and occupies an area that is only twice as large as Iran's. Iranian nationalism opposed Arab Nasserism: Iran sent troops to help the Royalists in North Yemen while Nasser helped the Arab nationalists trying to set up a republic. The shah was able to explain this action by maintaining that Nasserism was heavily influenced and even controlled by Soviet ideological imperatives, though Nasser's entire diplomatic record proved quite the contrary. The shah's high-handed, nationalist commitments compelled him to occupy three tiny, strategically important islands in the narrow entrance to the Persian Gulf (Abu Musa and the Tumbs). On November 30, 1971, the shah did his utmost to influence the Arab rulers of the Gulf littoral states from Oman to Kuwait.

The largest military operation in which Iranian forces were involved also took place in 1971. Iran sent troops to the sultan of Oman to put down the rebellion in Oman's southern province of Dhofar. The shah's greatest diplomatic maneuver came in 1955, when he adhered to the short-lived Baghdad Pact to form a "Northern Tier" alliance between Iran, Turkey, Pakistan, and Iraq (which Great Britain subsequently joined) as a defensive barrier to contain the USSR in the north, a kind of connecting link between NATO (North Atlantic Treaty Organization) in the West and SEATO (South East Asia Treaty Organization) in the East. As indicated earlier in this book, in 1958 Iraq withdrew from the pact; from then on it ceased to be called the Baghdad Pact and was renamed CENTO. The Central Treaty Organization, without Baghdad,[7] lasted until 1979, when Iran withdrew after the Islamic Revolution.

This leads us to the most critical issue in Iran's desire to dominate West

Asia: its rivalry in the region with Iraq. This rivalry appeared to end only when the shah and Saddam Hussein signed the Treaty of Algiers in 1975, reaching total agreement on all outstanding disputes. But these disputes, including the border demarcation of the Shatt-al-Arab river estuary, were far too deep to lay to rest with the mere stroke of a pen. While the Iran of the Pahlavis was a state purporting to national regeneration, it was not in the least inconsistent with the official religion of the nation: Shi'i Islam as opposed to Sunni Islam. The leaders of Iraq had always been Sunni Moslems ruling an Arab country that is predominantly (more than one-half) Shi'i. Iran under the shah was therefore not loath to play on Shi'i sentiments in the diplomatic disputes with Iraq that persisted up to 1975 and that were to reappear more vehemently when the Islamic Republic of Iran was established in 1979.

During the propaganda war between the two countries in the 1960s and 1970s, Iran identified Iraqi Sunni leadership with Yazid—the ruler of Iraq who, in the seventh century, killed Hossein, the grandson of the prophet Mohammad and one of the founders and martyred heroes of Shi'i Islam. It is in Iran's relations with Iraq that we clearly see how the ancient animosity between Arabs and Persians is directly transcended by their respective interpretations of Islam. On more than one occasion the Pahlavi monarch was implicated in several unsuccessful coups against the ruling Ba'ath regime in Iraq, and this occurred even before Khomeini called for the overthrow of Saddam Hussein.

"My enemy's enemy is my friend" is an old dictum that never escaped the attention of the Pahlavi ruler. The foregoing dictum is not only in reference to the Iraqi Kurds, whom the shah and the Iranian government assisted financially and militarily in their fight against the regime in Baghdad, but also, and more specifically, to the Israelis. This relationship with Israel goes as far back as 1950 (for some, all the way back to the *Book of Esther*), only two years after the establishment of *Eretz Yisrael*, when Iran extended to it a de facto recognition. A tacit understanding existed since then, with the implication that Iran was to dominate West Asia while Israel would remain supreme in the Middle East proper. Although this attitude to Israel changed somewhat after the 1967 and the 1973 wars, imperial Iran never did, not even when relations with Egypt had improved after 1973, endorse the idea of a Palestinian state. Countless Iranian officers received training in Israel or had visited that country. Both countries exchanged military supplies, and Israel's Mossad and Iran's Savak cooperated in the area of intelligence as far back as 1950. Israel's Mossad—together with America's CIA—helped train Savak operatives. Iran had in effect become Israel's chief supplier of oil. After the 1967 war, it was Iran that financed the Israeli-built 162-mile pipeline from Eilat on the Red Sea to Ashkelon on the Mediterranean.[8]

One of the most innovative features of the Pahlavi regime lies in the fact that Iranian foreign policy of this period was intent not so much on appropriating neighboring territory as much as it was on influencing it. The shah of Iran literally attempted to recreate a Persian empire the way Mussolini tried to resurrect a Roman one from Italy. Only Germany, Britain, and the Soviet Union had dared to do something similar in previous decades. But the latter were at least more advanced technologically and had larger populations and a tested military tradition. The shah probably realized the arduous task ahead of him. Since the land mass of western Asia is vast and sparsely populated, Iran entered the old Great Game by improving on the rail links of the Indo-Persian Corridor, the instrument of land penetration that the shah hoped would ultimately extend to the vast railway network of former British India. Railways in the developing world were, and are still, after all, the sinews of political and economic penetration. His father, Reza Shah, had, with the help of German engineers, been able to complete the fourteen hundred kilometer long Trans-Iranian Railway, which is a north-south line. What the son was striving for was an east-west line that would have redirected the flow of Afghan trade away from the Soviet border back to the markets of South Asia and the Middle East. To do this he had to link up the Iranian and Pakistani rail systems. Work finally began, and a spur from Qom, passing through Yazd, reached Kerman in 1977. The main Afghan cities—Herat, Kandahar, and Kabul—were supposed to be connected to this railroad, and it was thence to be extended to connect with China. The People's Republic of China had just been finishing the twelve hundred kilometer long Karakoram Highway crossing the Himalayas from Kashoger to Islamabad.[9] The Iranian dream was thus to establish a Teheran-Kabul-Islamabad (perhaps even a Beijing) axis and project Iranian influence over this new transportation infrastructure, an event of major geostrategic significance for both India and the USSR. Significantly, the shah actually gave Afghan president Mohammed Daoud a 2 billion dollar line of credit. What is noteworthy here is that Iraq did not figure in this projected infrastructure.

As a matter of fact, Iran was very upset over the recurring Indo-Pakistani wars, which drained Pakistan of resources more than it did India. He was likewise disillusioned with the CENTO alliance in that in a sense it pitted Pakistan against India. He was also dismayed with U.S. policies. In the first 1965 war between India and Pakistan, not only did the United States fail to assist Pakistan (a member of CENTO), but it actually refused to allow Iran to come to Pakistan's aid with arms purchased from the United States. The shah began to see his country as the linchpin of a Moslem, non-Arab alliance, with or without the support of the United States and Britain. In the wake of the Indo-Pakistan War of 1971, Iran publicly announced that it was opposed to any further weakening of Pakistan, from without or from within. There followed economic aid and military support to the Pakistani army in support of Pakistan's counterinsurgency campaign against the risings of the Baluch tribesmen in 1973.[10] The Pakistani province of Baluchistan borders on Iranian Baluchistan (where the Baluch are also a suppressed ethnic nationality) and imperial Iran was anxious that irredentism of this kind from neighboring countries would not spill over onto similar movements inside Iran. Iran invested heavily in Pakistan and India with a view to creating future sources of materials—consumer and otherwise—for an Iranian economic expansion that never really materialized.

It is a moot point, however, whether economic imperatives, especially those related to dwindling oil output, would have transformed the Iran of the shah into an even more aggressive power than it was. The views of the shah's critics (there were many of them at the time, and not only in left-wing circles) were simply not borne out in the shah's lifetime. For instance, before the fall of imperial Iran, Fred Halliday wrote:

From the mid-1980s onwards, as Iran's oil output falls, the temptation will be strong for Iran to make up for the fall in its domestic output by using its armed forces to seize the wells of neighbouring states, which still have considerable reserves and an income in excess of their requirements: Kuwait, Qatar and Saudi Arabia all fall into this category.[11]

Such prophetic words might have been imputed to the militaristic and police society of Iraq. In those days, however, was Iran genuinely the overwhelmingly powerful nation that so many have led us to believe? Iran had acquired more military hardware than it could possibly have used or even knew how to use. One wonders if in the shah's day a combined Arab force, equipped with Soviet and U.S. arms, could not have held their own against a supremely equipped Iranian army and navy? For the records all too eloquently indicate that the Iranian forces were primarily used to suppress the Iranian people, to discipline them, to be used as a show of force and maintain the Pahlavi dynasty in power. The mantle of would-be Iranian supremacy was destined to fall on Khomeini's Islamic Republic, in much the same way as Soviet Russia inherited much from tsarist Russia before it.

THE ISLAMIC REPUBLIC

The Iranian Revolution of 1979–1980 is now twelve years old. Under the guidance of Moslem fundamentalist Ayatollah Khomeini, Islam suddenly captured world attention. To understand why the revolution in Iran took place under the guise of religious fervor, it is necessary to examine the traditional role of religion in Iranian society and politics. Historically, the mosque maintained a close contact with the Iranian masses, and it served to channel criticism against unpopular monarchs, as was the case in the late 1970s. Now that the Iranian Islamic Republic has a constitution as well as a parliament (the Majlis) it is clear in what capacity this clergy has served.

But there was a difference between Khomeini's Iran and the shah's Iran. The creed of Ithna 'Ashari Shi'ism constituted that exceptional difference. Shi'ites throughout the centuries would regard as usurpers all the successors of Mohammad, whether Arab caliphs or Persian and Arab monarchs, recognizing only the descendants of Ali's (Mohammad's cousin and son-in-law) line as the "infallible" and "sinless" Imams. There were twelve such Imams; Khomeini himself was said to be a temporary incarnation of the last Imam, pending the Imam's second coming in the last Day of Judgment as the "Mahdi," a messiah of the world, who would come to redeem the faithful. In 1501, the Safavid dynasty established a new Iranian state and declared this Ithna 'Ashari form of Shi'ism to be the official religion of the state. But because Shi'i doctrine does not recognize temporal rulers as legitimate, it makes no separation between religion and politics. In this, Khomeini was at one with the founder of the Moslem Brotherhood, Hassan el-Banna, who said, "Islam is a home and a nationality, a religion and a state, a spirit and a word, and a book and a sword."

But the Shi'i perception of that fundamentalism went even further in its scheme of things. The ideology of the Islamic Republic of Iran was born of external as well as internal dimensions, just like the *Zahir* (exoteric) and *Batin* (esoteric) Shi'i precepts of this branch of Islam. The internal dimension is rooted in the fact that the Ithna 'Ashari Shi'i belief postulates that Islam is an impetus for evolution. For centuries the Shi'i sect of Islam had been the religion of dissent in Iran with the clergy acting as the most vocal opponents of unpopular monarchs; and because of persecution suffered at the hands of the Sunnis, the concept of martyrdom became deeply ingrained in the Iranian psyche. Externally, Shi'i Iran was regarded as fundamentally anti-Western. Iranian Shi'ism was then justifiably exportable to all other Moslem states, and primarily to all the secular states in the region, whether to a pseudo-socialist state like the Ba'athist regime in Iraq, or to military dictatorships using Islam as a pretext, like Pakistan. Khomeini had not only become leader of 100 million Shi'ites in the world; he had been designated by the Ithna 'Ashari Shi'i theory of government as the leader of all the 800 million Moslems in the world, comprising both Sunnis and Shi'ites. This precept was actually written into the Constitution of the Islamic Republic. Article 10 of that Constitution reads:

All Moslems form a single nation, and the Government of the Islamic Republic of Iran has the duty of formulating its general policies with a view to the merging and union of all Moslem peoples, and it must constantly strive to bring about the political, economic and cultural unity of the Islamic world.[12]

In foreign policy, in particular, this theocratic worldview amounted to a rejection of the contemporary international system as it existed. To deal with that system, however, Iran had, as one analyst aptly put it, brought about "a deliberate transformation of the major alignments of Iran's foreign relations as they existed previously."[13] According to Professor Rouholla K. Ramazani, Khomeini's worldview was based on six general principles: (a) no dependence on East or West (b) regard of the United States as the main enemy (c) continuous struggle against the Zionist power (d) the liberation of Jerusalem (e) anti-imperialism, and, most important of all, (f) support for all oppressed peoples everywhere, and particularly for Moslems.[14]

There was evidently an element of populism, even a strain of socialism, in references to oppressed peoples. The Soviet Union was in effect never depicted as negatively as the United States. Although there may have been a convergence of views between Iran and the USSR in regard to the "imperialism" of the Western powers, the Soviet Union never considered itself culturally "anti-Western," which was patently the case with Iran. Nor will Shi'ism acknowledge the Marxist division of the world into socialist and capitalist states. It refers, instead, to the traditional Islamic division of the world into *dar al-Islam* (house of Islam) and *dar al-harb* (house of war).

But nowhere does Shi'ism apply more critically than in regard to the Arab states, to those of the Gulf in particular. In the Iranian mind, these states had defected from true Islam. From the very outset, Ayatollah Montazeri, Khomeini's one-time religious successor, explained Iran's attitude to other Moslems thus:

One of the characteristics of Iran's Islamic Revolution is that its mundane scope cannot be confined to certain geographical and continental areas. Indeed, our revolution is an Islamic revolution, not an Iranian revolution.... Final victory will be achieved when there is no trace of colonialism and exploitation left throughout the entire Islamic world.... All Muslims and defenceless persons in the world who are living under dictatorship and colonialism have certain expectations from the Muslim nation of Iran, and our glorious revolution is duty-bound toward these people. The Iranian government and people, to the extent they can, must give material and psychological support and assistance to all freedom movements, especially to the Palestinian revolution.[15]

These remarks were made in the year of Khomeini's accession to power. In February 1979, Yasir Arafat, leader of the Palestine Liberation Organization (PLO) had been the first foreign dignitary to officially visit the Islamic Republic. Khomeini's good-will gesture to Arafat was to allow him to expropriate the vacated Israeli embassy in Teheran.

However, when war broke out between Iran and Iraq in September 1980, Arafat suddenly found that he had to choose between his allegiance to the Arab nationalism of an emerging Iraq and his sympathy for the Islamic Revolution. It was not really a difficult decision for a Palestinian nationalist to make. Few Palestinians (except those rioting against Israeli administration in the Gaza Strip and the West Bank) were ever sympathetic to Iranian Shi'ism. Many Palestinians volunteered to fight on the Iraqi side; and it came as no surprise in the end when Arafat abandoned his short-lived alliance with Khomeini. Since then, the PLO has been in conflict with nearly all the fundamentalist Moslem groups. Khomeini belatedly realized that Arafat's objective chiefly lay in the creation of a secular Palestinian state. In Lebanon, for instance, pro-Khomeini Shi'i militiamen have been fiercely battling PLO forces; in early 1985 Shi'i forces loyal to the Lebanese Hizb'Allah (the Party of God) made an aborted attempt to destroy the PLO camps in the Beirut area. Throughout Lebanon, Hizb'Allah's exploits have included kidnappings of Americans and Europeans, suicide attacks, hijackings: Witness the case of the Air Afrique jet when a French passenger was murdered in July 1987. It was reported at this time that Khomeini "spends anywhere from $15 million to $50 million a year to finance Hizb'Allah activities in Lebanon."[16]

In addition to Lebanon, the Iranians were adroitly exploiting their kinship with the Shi'i minorities of the Gulf Arab states: Kuwait, 30–40 percent; Dubai, 30 percent; Qatar, 20 percent. More important to Teheran are the Gulf states where the Shi'ites constitute one-half of the whole population or where they are an actual majority but living under a Sunni government: Oman, 50 percent; Iraq, 60 percent; Bahrain, 75 percent, not to mention Lebanon again, where Shi'ites today are more numerous than Sunni Moslems and the Maronite and Orthodox Christians. To all these Shi'i elements Iran had made repeated calls to rise in revolt against their "illegitimate" Sunni governments.

The subversive methods Iran employed became the subject of the world's headlines. In some Gulf states agents of the Islamic Republic set up secret cells known as Hussainiyyas, which masqueraded as religious study groups. Sometimes they went unnoticed, escaping the vigilant eye of the local police; sometimes they were detected by the Arab security agencies and suppressed. Iran was already on record for trying to overthrow the Bahrain government in December of 1981, and it was responsible for an abortive coup in Qatar in the autumn of 1983. In September 1982, an Iranian Shi'i leader, Hujjat Al-Islam Musavi Khuayni, led a group of Shi'ites to Mecca during the ceremonial *Hajj* and publicly announced that his goal was to dispose of the "corrupt" Saudi royal family. A much larger variation on the same theme occurred in the first week of August 1987, when thousands of Iranian pilgrims rioted and attempted to seize the Sacred Mosque at Mecca; their aim was to topple the Sunni-ruled kingdom and proclaim Khomeini the leader of all Islam. The bid was foiled by Saudi security forces (possibly with the assistance of U.S. military and naval intelligence); but the event left well over four hundred persons dead, and Saudi-Iranian relations soured to the point where the Saudis, helpless and bewildered, decided it was time to cut all diplomatic ties with Teheran.

Not surprisingly, the most novel aspect of the Iranian revolution (in addition to the Soviet invasion of Afghanistan, of course) is that it inflicted the final blow to CENTO. The shah himself had many misgivings about this alliance. The threat of an exportable Ithna 'Ashari Shi'i led to the establishment in 1981 of the Gulf Cooperation Council (GCC), a kind of collective security belt composed of Saudi Arabia, Bahrain, Oman, Kuwait, Qatar, and the United Arab Emirates. The GCC's defense budget rose above 40 billion dollars per year, which included U.S. AWAC planes and other sophisticated military equipment totaling more than half of what the whole Third World earmarks for defense spending. Nevertheless, this whole outlay for the GCC was still no deterrent to the Iranian threat, or to an Iraqi one later on. The only state seriously concerned about it was Israel. Strategic planners in the United States had long since recognized that, barring Iraq, the only viable deterrent against Iran in the Persian Gulf was and remains the U.S. Rapid Deployment Joint Task Force (RDF), which in January 1983 had been renamed the U.S. Central Command, or USCENTCOM—with a power-projection second only to NATO in Europe.[17]

What is surprising, however, was Iran's relationship with Syria, an Arab country ruled by Moslem Alawites who trace their allegiance to Ismailism, one of the offshoots of the Shi'i movement. Syrian Alawites therefore had had more affinity with the Shi'ites in Iran than with Sunni Arabs elsewhere. But Syria is, above all, a nationalist Arab country ruled by a single-party Ba'athist regime. No doubt too, Syria's rivalry with Iraq had brought it closer to Iran and, together with Libya, it was the only Arab country supporting the Iranian war effort. Many were of the opinion that Iran maintained friendly ties only to those Arab countries who belonged to the "rejectionist front" in relation to Israel. This is still the case. But the Syrian-Iranian relationship cannot be pigeon-holed so simply. Syria, after all, has had its own problems with Moslem fundamentalists, such as the Moslem Brotherhood. Why, then, should Syria, both when the war was going in Iran's favor and then when Iranian fortunes were down, have wanted a fundamentalist regime in Iraq? The Syrians had themselves fought and reportedly cleared the Bekaa Valley of Khomeini supporters[18]—the Hizb'Allah Party. In mid-August 1987, in a conciliatory gesture to the United States, the Syrians helped free the U.S. journalist Charles Glass from his Shi'i kidnappers. This is not to say that Hafez Assad of Syria was ever ready to change sides in the Iran-Iraq war out of a sudden, belated recognition of a vague commitment to the Arab cause. His ties with Iran had been of a purely practical nature: Syria was receiving special concessions on oil purchases in Iran.

Now that the Iranian-Iraqi war and Saddam's war over Kuwait are behind us, Syria may be loosening its ties with Iran. First there is the lingering problem that rival Shi'i militias battled for West Beirut's southern slums. With its proxy, "Amal," Syria was trying to gain control of these southern suburbs in order to maintain credibility in Lebanon, a country Damascus has so far considered well within its sphere of influence. But Iran, even after the war with Iraq, may be all the more determined to support Hizb'Allah, the only organization that had gained a significant foreign foothold for Iran's Islamic Revolution. If that should come to pass, Syria and Iran could come to a complete parting of the ways. Syria may even be compelled to use the same scorched-earth tactics it used to quell fundamentalist dissenters in Hamra, inside Syria, where, when it all ended, fifteen thousand people had been murdered by Syrian government troops.

THE GULF WAR

The most dramatic impact on the Great Game in the region as it was being played out by the regional powers was the seemingly endless war with Iraq. After eight years this war exceeded in casualties all the Arab-Israeli wars combined, ranking sixth in terms of damage and death among all interstate wars in the world since 1815. Iraq decidedly started the conflict with a preemptive strike in September 1980. But this came about as a result of Iran's calling on the Shi'ites in Iraq to revolt and overthrow the Ba'ath government and the ruling *Tekriti* clique of Saddam Hussein. The Voice of Revolutionary Iran often exhorted the more than five million "sons of Ali to rise up against the sons of Yazid," invocations reminiscent of Iranian propaganda at the time of the shah. Financial assistance was sent to the al-Da'wa underground Shi'i movement in Iraq. In 1980 members of the al-Da'wa tried to assassinate Tariq Aziz, Iraq's foreign minister. All the Arab Gulf states that were bankrolling Iraq—primarily Saudi Arabia and Kuwait—and those that sent pilots and arms (Jordan, Egypt) likewise became the targets of Iran's fury. The war was thus never confined to the battlefields along their common border; rather, it was carried on by proxy to Lebanon, Abu Dhabi, Turkey, Libya, even to Paris and London.

The Saudis and their Arab allies were coordinating their OPEC oil-price stance at meetings of the Arab League heads-of-government, where Iran was repeatedly condemned for occupying Iraqi territory. At the important Arab summit in Algiers in June 1988, the leaders declared that the twenty-one member Arab League was in total solidarity with Iraq and its defense of its national territories. Alone among the Arabs, only Syria raised an objection, but it did so rather mildly.

For the duration of the Iran-Iraq war, Iran did not have much of a dialogue, nor any diplomatic contacts for that matter, with any Arab state except Libya, Algeria, and Syria. Its ties with Pakistan were tenuous at best; it tolerated but never actually recognized the Soviet-supported Marxist regime in Afghanistan. Although there are many Shi'ites living in Afghanistan's border region of Herat, the population of Afghanistan is for the most part Sunni. In the eighteenth century the Iranian Safavid dynasty had been temporarily overthrown by an invasion of Afghans who tried to impose Sunnism on Iran—an event that was not forgotten by the Shi'i leadership that considered Afghan refugees in Iran third-class citizens. But we have been wrongly led to believe that the Shi'i regime was absolutely incapable of evolution from within, or impervious to change from without. There is every reason to believe otherwise. Let us examine the evidence.

First, the internal situation in Iran was never an optimistic one. There was high inflation; rampant corruption had reached intolerable proportions; food, fuel, and electricity were in short supply; and defections and treason in the military were numerous. The general dissatisfaction with the war was obvious, although by the summer of 1988, even when things were taking a bad turn, the Iranian Central Bank still had more than 5.1 billion dollars in foreign reserves with which to finance that war and import consumer goods. But oil revenues go up and down as the international market dictates. For Iran this was not good. The only pariah in the region, the country could obtain nothing on credit. Second, Iraq's superiority over Iran in military hardware at the time was approximately five to one. Third, there was a fierce power struggle in the government between the moderates and the hard-liners, between Ayatollah Montazeri on the one hand (who was supported in 1986 by Hashemi and the Revolutionary Guards) and Hojatolislam Hashemi Rafsanjani—the then speaker of the Parliament—on the other. After the revelations and scandal that erupted in connection with the secret McFarlane mission to Teheran in 1986, and indirect bargaining with the United States and Israel for necessary military equipment and spare parts, the more moderate Rafsanjani publicly declared:

There are at present two relatively powerful factions in our country with differences of view on how the country should be run and on the role of the government and that of the private sector in affairs. These two tendencies also exist in the Majlis, in the government, within the clergy, within the universities and across society as a whole.... They may in fact be regarded as two parties without names.[19]

Already in 1986 there were many in Teheran who felt that for the sake of the war some secret accommodation might be reached with the United States out of sheer necessity. Khomeini, however, reacted angrily and began supporting the hard-liners in this internal struggle. In the first half of 1987, Khomeini was still capable of running the country. His will was obeyed. The Iranians were very capable of playing a double game, as the following episode will convey, when Iranian pilgrims rioted in Saudi Arabia.

Not fanaticism, to be sure, but an astute example of histrionics grandiloquently characterized the Shi'i riots in Mecca in the summer of 1987. No doubt Khomeini mounted this spectacle to deflect public opinion from internal problems and to help cement the unity of the country. It was the Iranian way of dealing with crisis management. Consider for a moment how propaganda might effectively create in the public mind a chronic sense of crisis during the Mecca pilgrimage. Then the state shows its mettle and

determination by taking bold and decisive actions (i.e., war games in the
Gulf code-named "martyrdom"), displaying its own kind of brinkmanship.
According to a prominent Western observer, "The revolutionary regime in
Teheran aspires, as did the Shah before it, to be recognized as the dominant
power of the region.... Iran's tactical performance has been shrewd and
tough. The new regime has used whatever leverage available to seize the
initiative and to keep its many adversaries off balance."[20] Interestingly,
most other Western commentators, who persistently ignored the relationship between internal conditions and external actions, seemed to believe
that when Iran acted pragmatically it acted realistically, adopting a pro-
Western, pro-American attitude. That is how Rafsanjani's pro-U.S. lobby
was usually explained. But the only noticeable pragmatism that one was
able to detect among the Iranians is the ability to play one power off against
another, a constant in the behavior of any small, Third World nation, so
often subordinated to foreign influences and powers in the past. Again, this
was a small power's response to the Great Game that it usually saw being
played by colonial masters.

It should be pointed out that Teheran had astutely signed an important
trade pact that included a sizable arms deal with China for the sale of
tanks, planes, and Silkworm missiles and spare parts. It was a desperate
move; no one else was willing to sell them weapons any more. Then there
came a new period of friendliness toward Moscow, around the beginning
of 1987. But the turning point did not come until February 1986, with the
arrival in Teheran of Georgi Kornienko (first deputy foreign minister) to
begin talks on natural gas deliveries and to establish an Aeroflot route
between the Iranian capital and Moscow. That visit was reciprocated by
the Iranian foreign minister, Ali Akbar Velayati, in February 1987. Amid the
upheavals of August 1987, Soviet deputy foreign minister Yuli Vorontsov
visited Teheran and asked that Iran stop obstructing the search for a
negotiated settlement of the Afghan crisis. He intimated that in return, the
USSR would not support a UN resolution that would impose sanctions or
a global arms embargo against Iran if Iran failed to observe a cease-fire in
the Iran-Iraq war. Considering that four years previously Iran had suppressed the Communist Tudeh Party, jailing or executing the local communist leaders, this rapprochement with Moscow came as a surprise.
Warming up to the Soviets allowed Iran to procrastinate on any new UN
Security Council resolution and Secretary-General Perez de Cuellar's efforts
to end the war.[21] For as long as it could, Iran tried to continue the war for
both national and religious reasons, and consequently did not want to be
cut off from potential arms suppliers. The Soviet news agency, TASS, repeatedly announced that "Moscow and Teheran are mutually concerned
over the unprecedented buildup of the U.S. military presence in the region."
And, if anything, Moscow reacted strongly to the Iraqi resumption of the
tanker war in the fall of 1987.

Iran and the Soviet Union then began to reopen oil pipelines, and their talks centered on building a second rail link from Iran to Soviet Central Asia. Because of the Gulf War, Iran expanded port facilities at Bandar Abbas and at Shah Bahar. Teheran even took up the Pahlavi monarch's railway schemes and expressed an interest in establishing a rail link to Bandar Abbas, either from Kerman or Bafq, over a distance of roughly 750 kilometers. (Work is currently moving ahead along the Bam-Shur Gaz alignment toward Zaheday.)[22] Again, as in the days of the shah—though not for the same reasons—this was probably motivated by geostrategic expedience: to bring Iran closer to an Asian infrastructure and to Asian markets rather than to the West, thus utilizing to its fullest the advantages of its geographical location. Possibly, too, Iran was turning toward the USSR for another reason: Over the previous five years Pakistan had been receiving more than 3 million dollars in U.S. military and economic aid, becoming the most important U.S. ally in Southwest Asia. There was some talk that Pakistan was toying with the possibility of giving the United States airbases in Pakistan's province of Baluchistan, together with the use of port facilities near Karachi.[23] In such a scenario Pakistan would emerge as something of a proxy fighting force in the Gulf, a vital link in the entire USCENTCOM defense perimeter, a point that further threatened the basic commitments of the Iranian Revolution.

Yet not all Iranians reacted this way to Pakistan. Many moderates felt that precisely because of Pakistan's growing importance to the region, partly too, because Pakistan now possessed the bomb, there ought to be some sort of partnership between Islamabad and Teheran. True, Pakistan is Sunni, Iran is Shi'i; but the "creature" of the "Great Satan," which the Iranians usually ascribed to Pakistan, is a country that is more like the Middle East than the Indian subcontinent. True, many Pakistanis living near Iran's border speak Farsi, curiously drawn to the splendor of a superior Persian culture. These Iranians reasoned that Pakistan's contribution to a powerful Pakistan-Iran, Moslem non-Arab axis would be technological expertise. But this assistance was again all related to the war effort against Iraq, an effort which, in view of U.S. support for Iraq, was already beginning to fall apart in early 1988, and with it, the fortunes of war, not to mention Shi'i supremacy in the whole region.

THE UNITED STATES SIDES WITH THE ARABS

Initially, the U.S. government had maintained a strict neutrality in the Iran-Iraq conflict. Public opinion in the United States, on the other hand, was rabidly anti-Iranian from the very start of the war. Still fresh in the United States was the memory of nightly television coverage of surging anti-American crowds in the early days of the revolution. Americans remembered how the Iranians, breaching international law and protocol, held more than fifty persons of the U.S. embassy hostage for over a year. Faced with the likelihood of an Iranian victory spilling over to the friendly Arab states of the Gulf, U.S. officials began to take better stock of the situation. Moreover, the leaders of the six-nation GCC, which met in Riyadh in early January 1988, decided to coordinate their defense strategies and appealed to the Americans for help.

There was an all-out panic in the Gulf when Iran began launching Chinese-built Silkworm missiles against Kuwait, a member of the GCC. At the GCC summit, King Fahd of Saudi Arabia reportedly said that the Iranians "were pointing their arrows to our chests instead of helping us to liberate Jerusalem from Zionist domination. There is no reasonable justification for this other than the desire for expansion."[24] The situation was becoming so serious that the Gulf Council raised the possibility of direct Egyptian military assistance, given the newly established solidarity between Egypt and the Arab states.[25] It seemed that the whole world was ostracizing Iran for not complying with UN Resolution 598, which called upon the belligerents to agree to a cease-fire. In late December 1987 all the members of the UN Security Council, including China and the Soviet Union, signed a statement saying they would impose an arms embargo if Iran did not comply. Work on a draft of the actual embargo resolution was in fact expected to begin in late January 1988. But that never got anywhere; resolutions, the Iranians argued, were only pieces of paper, and Iran was not fooled. Behind the scenes, the Soviet Union was making a bid to get into the act; it made a direct proposal to the Reagan administration. It was suggested that both the Soviets and the Americans would enforce the embargo under UN auspices, primarily by blockading the entire Gulf region. The White House rejected the idea. It obviously involved an increased Soviet presence in the Gulf, and that was regarded by the Pentagon and the State Department as an overt threat to U.S. interests. The Arabs, as indicated, still preferred the stationing of Egyptian troops; but short of helping the Iraqis with pilot training, Egypt refused to have anything to do with the Persian Gulf.[26]

The United States Supports Iraq in the Iran-Iraq War

It is at this point, in February 1988, that the U.S. government, without making the issue formal and public, decided to throw in its lot with Iraq. Until further evidence is furnished to prove otherwise, here at least is how I would reconstruct the sequence of events—presented here in a somewhat fragmented form—that took place in that year and led me to this compelling conclusion.

On several occasions, throughout the 1980s, President Saddam Hussein of Iraq expressed his interest in expanding diplomatic contacts with the United States. The Reagan administration responded positively to these overtures, and in 1984 diplomatic relations between Washington and Baghdad were reestablished. Iraq was then immediately removed from the list of countries accused of aiding and abetting terrorism, and without much further ado—there was sporadic criticism of this development within Congress—all U.S. restrictions on exports to Iraq were lifted. In fact, when the existence of Iraq as a state was at risk, Saddam Hussein made every effort to emphasize to the U.S. government the value of his regime's survival. France, too, had been supporting the Iraqi war effort with Etendard fighter planes, and thus Paris had an interest in preventing an Iraqi military defeat. But, by and large, it was the United Sates of America that was becoming Iraq's protector. As early as 1984, Iraq was receiving intelligence information from U.S. satellites passing over the battlefronts and from Saudi Arabian AWACS. There was no secret about this. In a book written by Shahram Chubin and Charles Tripp, *Iran and Iraq at War* (1988), there are many direct and subtle references to this U.S. interference. Nor is any evidence lacking in support of the argument that the Iraqis began using poison gas against the Iranian offensives, also as early as 1984, and then again in 1985 and 1986. The UN Security Council was the first to condemn the use of chemical weapons by Iraq in 1986, even though at that time Iraq was clearly on the defensive. Journalists, commentators, Middle East analysts—so shamelessly anti-Iranian during the Gulf War—downplayed the help Iraq had been receiving from the Americans.

Feeling emboldened, with Egyptian backing and Saudi and Kuwaiti financing, Saddam Hussein decided that Iraq should finally move to the offensive in early 1988. A conference debating this subject was actually held in Baghdad.[27] At the end of February, the Iraqi foreign minister, Tariq Aziz, asked the United States to delay any diplomatic action designed to impose an arms embargo. Iraq then began pressing its "war of the cities," with constant missile barrages lasting from late February until mid-April. The demonstrated superiority in missile stockpiles during the last round of this exchange paid off for Iraq. Iran stopped its own missile attacks on Baghdad and gave up the long-range artillery attacks against Basra, the Iraqi strategic city in the south that Iran had failed to capture in 1987 after several human-wave offensives that cost more than eighty thousand lives.

The next step in the Iraqi strategic plan was to launch a series of offensives in order to regain all the territory occupied by Iran. But this could not have been accomplished without careful military planning in logistics and intelligence gathering, which seems to suggest that Iraq could not have brought off its startling victories without the United States providing the Iraqi army the necessary satellite intelligence that helped turn the tide against attacking Iranian forces. Surprisingly, the Iraqi ground attack aimed at regaining the Fao Peninsula also coincided with the heaviest fighting between U.S. naval forces and Iran in the Gulf. While the Iraqis were recapturing the Fao Peninsula (April 18) after only thirty-four hours of fighting, the United States Navy attacked two Iranian oil platforms, disabled two Iranian frigates, and sank at least four gunboats. While this was going on, Iran claimed that U.S. helicopters were helping Iraqi troops on Fao. Iran launched missiles against U.S. warships in what appeared to be a simultaneous two-front battle, one on land, the other at sea. From then on there followed a string of Iraqi attacks on Iranian positions leading to the recapture on May 25 of Iraqi territory east of Basra near Shalamcheh, after only nine hours of fighting, and the recapture on June 25 of the oil-rich Majnoon Islands after only eight hours of fighting.[28]

Having pushed Iran from virtually all significant Iranian footholds in southern Iraq, the better-equipped, better-trained, and now more highly motivated Iraqi armed forces—spearheaded by the ninety-thousand man elite Republican Guard—had no problems in reconquering Iraq's northern Kurdish area to force the last major concentration of Iranian troops and to liberate the Kurdish town of Halabja, where the Iraqis resorted to chemical weapons. Thus developments on the war front in 1988 had all favored Iraq.

Iranian Overtures to the United States

Realizing that a rapprochement with the Soviet Union was not enough, that to win the war against Iraq, relations with the United States must somehow also be normalized and restored, the more moderate faction in Iran made repeated overtures to U.S. State Department officials in an effort to reestablish some dialogue. This took place over the same six-month period in which U.S. policy was tilting toward Iraq, from about the end of December 1987 until just before the sad destruction of the Iranian airliner by the U.S. cruiser *Vincennes* in July 1988.

There was an intermediary in these Iranian initiatives, an Iranian-American scholar (identity unknown) who maintained that there were three such probes made by Iran; the first two were rejected by suspicious U.S. officials in the State Department, and the third overture simply collapsed. The *Los Angeles Times*, which had come to know about them, was soon able to report: "The fruitless effort to establish a dialogue between the United States and Iran has been marked by misunderstandings, missed opportunities and suspicion on the part of American officials badly burned in the Iran-Contra scandal."[29]

Government officials in the United States warned Teheran that because of former White House aide Oliver North's abortive negotiations with Iran in the past, any future dialogue could not remain confidential. The Iranians wanted to keep the talks secret. One of the contacts through the go-between was Iran's deputy foreign minister himself, Mohammad Javad Larijani. But the Reagan administration shrugged him off out of fear that he was acting either on his own or as an ally of Hashemi Rafsanjani. He was not considered a representative of the entire Khomeini regime. Some months later, however, Rafsanjani became commander-in-chief of the Iranian armed forces in addition to retaining his official title as speaker of Iran's Parliament. It almost seemed that U.S. decision makers did not wish to parley with the Iranians at all. Another envoy described by the Iranian-American middle-man was a confidential adviser to Khomeini and Rafsanjani, a man referred to as "Rafsanjani's Kissinger."[30] He held a doctorate in political science from the Sorbonne; but, as it happened, the Americans mistook him for an anti-Western radical who had been expelled from France, refusing to grant him a visa to come to Washington. He, too, had been sent by Rafsanjani to open a narrow channel of communication with the U.S. government before Khomeini died.[31]

This is not to say that the Reagan administration never wanted to parley with the Iranian regime. The problem in the State Department, as well as on Capitol Hill, was, rather: To whom could one, or should one, speak in Iran? The Iran-Contra scandal showed up all too well how Reagan and his security advisers had wanted to do something for Iran in 1985–1986, when a working relationship with Iranian moderates resulted in the United States sending arms to Iran in exchange for hostages. Doing business of this type ended in disaster, shaking the U.S. security establishment to its foundations and making a mockery of U.S. policies that tried to buy the good will of the Iranians by rewarding kidnappers with secret ransom.

In an article in the *New York Times* of April 15, 1991, Gary Sick pointed out that former President Ronald Reagan and his running-mate George Bush were involved in a secret deal on the hostages during the 1980 crisis. The secret deal was allegedly negotiated between William Casey, then Mr. Reagan's campaign chairman, and Mehdi Karrubi, one of Khomeini's representatives, at a Madrid hotel in July, 1980. Gary Sick contends that there was a deal to delay the release of the hostages purposely until after the American election on November 4th. Meetings concerning this issue were held in Paris in October of that year. At one of these meetings George Bush was allegedly present. Teheran agreed to release the fifty-two hostages five minutes after Mr. Reagan took the oath of office; and arms started to flow to Iran by way of Israel only a few days after Mr. Reagan's inauguration. For the record, the White House has denied these allegations, and today the official version is that Mr. Bush never went to Paris for any secret deal with the Iranians.

A CRITIQUE OF U.S. POLICIES IN THE GULF

My general conclusion regarding U.S. involvement in the Gulf is that, at best, it was hazardous (witness the problems associated with escorting Kuwaiti oil tankers out of the Gulf and sweeping the waters for mines laid by Iran), and at worst, it was a dangerously irresponsible policy.

The Persian Gulf and the narrow Strait of Hormuz are not U.S. waterways:

They are sea lanes leading to the Indian Ocean. In the crucible of war that pitted Iran against Iraq, a number of things went wrong that ought not to have embroiled the United States Navy at all. The argument that the Americans were protecting the southern Gulf's Arab shaykdoms, to my mind, is not a convincing one. Nor is the argument that without USCENTCOM's presence (note that at that time 20 million dollars a month was being spent for the Gulf deployment), the Soviets would long have seized the oilfields and warm-water ports of the Gulf.

The U.S. naval presence in the region at the time was well beyond that maintained by any other nation. Before Iraq invaded Kuwait, the U.S. deployment consisted of one command ship, four destroyers or frigates, one cruiser, and four escorts for the cruiser. There was also an aircraft carrier group from *Diego Garcia* in the Indian Ocean in case of an emergency requiring sustained air support. The French, the British, and the Italians were there in far-reduced numbers. By contrast, in this decade and in the last the Soviets have had no large warships in the Gulf at all, save one or two frigates for reconnaissance to monitor U.S. activities and for minesweeping operations, although most of Iraq's weapons were Soviet-built and sold by the Soviet Union.

By early 1988 the first Gulf War had already taken on all the features of a high-speed, high-tech video game. In order to protect the sea lanes and those reflagged Kuwaiti tankers, almost every day unidentified boats and aircraft, rapidly moving blips on a radar screen, were challenged by U.S. men-of-war. These warships would force them to respond, to state their intentions, warning that failure to do so would put their aircraft at great peril. That became the essence and justification of U.S. defensive measures. That precisely was what had happened to the Iranian passenger plane with civilians on board, an aircraft that was following a regular flight schedule and flying within its own air corridor.

The Aegis System, an ultrasophisticated electronic command and control system, which the cruiser *Vincennes* was using to detect the civil jet transport, mistook it for a hostile Iranian F-14 jet fighter and shot it out of the sky. Americans, afterwards, were asking themselves what had gone wrong with the Aegis System. This was America's reply to the consequences of a tragic accident. President Reagan himself stated in no ambiguous terms that the United States Navy's error in shooting down the airliner was somewhat more reasonable than the Soviet mistake in shooting down a Korean passenger airliner in 1983.[32] The U.S. government was spending billions of dollars on exotic weapons—considered by many as foolproof in the science of war—and very few in the administration could bring themselves to acknowledge not only that a U.S. "star-wars-at-sea" armada should be brought into question but that the moral standards of U.S. involvement were seriously flawed, that U.S. policies in the Gulf were awkward and incoherent.

To add insult to injury, George Bush, just three and a half months away
from the U.S. election, called Iran a "barbaric nation" at the UN Security
Council in the aftermath of the tragedy designed to determine the extent
of U.S. responsibility. The *New York Times* columnist William Safire explained away the *Vincennes*'s captain's decision to fire the missiles as the
only possible course of action in view of the stressful "pucker factor"—to
which he the captain was supposedly subjected—mindful, no doubt, of the
thirty-seven U.S. sailors who died when the frigate *Stark* had been acci-
dentally attacked by an Iraqi jet in 1987.[33] Conspiracy theorists even blamed
Iran for the air disaster, morbidly suggesting that the Iranian aircraft had
been stuffed with naked bodies and then aimed toward the *Vincennes* in a
bid to get itself shot down, Kamikaze-fashion.[34] Another far-fetched theory
was advanced by Neil Livingstone, president of the Institute of Terrorism
and Subnational Conflict, who said that the Iranians had actually "doctored
the crash site to produce quick, vivid pictures."[35] Within two years of this
incident, the United States decided to award a medal to the captain of the
USS *Vincennes*.

IRAN PURSUES THE PRAGMATIC LINE

The predictable cries for revenge, to be sure, reverberated across Iran.
But despite the air tragedy, Iranian leaders never ruled out the possibility
of accepting U.N. Resolution 598. Iran simply could not and did not confront
the U.S. fleet directly. Moreover, Rafsanjani showed extraordinary restraint
in his public pronouncements after the tragedy. In an attempt to break
Iran out of its international isolation, Rafsanjani set about garnering sympathy for the Iranian cause as the victim of U.S. aggression, saying that
Iran had often made enemies needlessly. At the same time friendly gestures,
which had been cut short by the aircraft disaster, were eagerly pursued in
the form of improved contact with the West, notably Britain and France.
Then, on July 18, 1988, came another surprise: Iran finally accepted the
terms of the UN cease-fire resolution, Resolution 598. Within a matter of
hours the Iranian leadership announced the resumption of diplomatic relations with Canada, which had also been severed for eight years.[36] Re-
newing its relationship with Canada was widely seen as an effort by Teheran
to negotiate with the United States.

At this point we should stop to ask ourselves: What combination of forces
was at work that prompted Iran to comply with the cease-fire resolutions
and bring an end to the war? Was it Khomeini's impending death? Was it
entirely due to Iraq's battle successes on the ground, or was it the Iranian
public's lackluster support for Khomeini's war effort? Could one not point
to a delaying tactic by Teheran's leadership? Certainly U.S. administration
officials could gloatingly claim that Iran's turnabout vindicated the decision

by both Washington and the other Western naval powers to build up their Gulf fleets.

But there was no longer any doubt about Iranian intentions when Khomeini himself made the decision to extricate his country from the war. "Making this decision was more deadly than drinking poison," the Imam reportedly said. According to U.S. intelligence sources, on the evening of July 16 there was a meeting in Teheran of senior political officials, including Montazeri, Rafsanjani, Prime Minister Mir Hussein Mousavi, and Ahmed Khomeini, the Ayatollah's oldest son. Montazeri supported Rafsanjani, recommending that in the interests of the revolution, the elder Khomeini should confirm the Iranian leadership's agreement to a cease-fire. Khomeini's announcement was welcomed in every Arab capital of the Middle East, albeit with caution. Only Israel voiced misgivings about an end to the fighting between its two implacable foes: Iraq and Iran.

It somehow seemed unlike Iran to want suddenly to put an end to the war, and if Iran needed a respite—which many Arab leaders claimed it was trying to do—this was a sure way of going about it. Even while negotiations were proceeding as to the type of U.N.-monitored cease-fire to be put in place, it did not take long for hostilities to break out again, and the din of battle would not subside until the two felt they had gained enough leverage in the peace negotiations. In a keynote address to the Iranian Parliament, Rafsanjani raised the prospect, somewhat ambiguously, of a new relationship with the United States, suggesting that Iran would be willing to help secure the release of nine U.S. hostages held by pro-Iranian factions in Lebanon. That, too, ought to have been interpreted as another overture to Washington. Rafsanjani qualified the statement by saying that the Americans should free Iranian assets that were held in the United States for a decade, including 400 million dollars worth of armaments still left undelivered to Iran during that period. This should have been seen as a clear illustration that despite all the rhetoric about the "Great Satan," Iran was ready to mend fences and seek some accommodation with the United States.

I would carry on with the story of America's reluctance to speak with the Iranians—but that story is best told in the way the Americans ignored the new threat to the Gulf from Iraq. I will even add that the Americans themselves had a hand in the invasion of Kuwait. I implore the reader to bear with me; I shall deal extensively with this issue toward the end, in the chapter on Iraq.

Let me conclude by saying that Iran's threat to its neighboring Gulf states has always been somewhat of an exaggeration. With U.S. support, the combined effort of CENTCOM and the GCC was enough to deter any exalted Iranian adventurism or alleged Soviet ambitions in the Gulf. The United States has in the last few years encouraged joint exercise and joint defense efforts by the GCC. Saudi Arabia has an AWAC-supported air defense system. In addition, the Reagan administration had bolstered Turkey's defenses by helping that country—and 7 billion dollars a year is no small sum—to modernize its airfields and to build new ones at Batman and Mus in eastern Anatolia. Thus NATO contingencies were now likewise tied to the security of the Persian Gulf. Apparently, and here is the rub, Washington did not believe that all these measures were quite enough to deter Iran's continued advance in Iraq in 1987, or else it would not have lent significant support to Iraq in 1988.

Some questions regarding military tactics still linger in my mind, however: Why did Iran not try to open another front against Iraq by attacking that country from across the Syrian border, to which Iraq had sent only 100,000 troops, a number insufficient to hold down a massive attack over very extensive lines of communications? The Iraqis would have been overwhelmed and forced to shift fresh troops from the south to that new and far weaker front.

A more rational player in such a game of power politics and regional alliances, when the stakes are stacked against him, would not have eschewed military cooperation with a state like Israel, whose enemies have traditionally been the same as Iran's: In vain the Israelis made several overtures to the Iranians to assist them in their struggle against Iraq. The Israelis had always attempted to form something of a tacit Israel–Iran–Saudi Arabia alliance, trying to involve the less credulous Americans in this scheme. Back in October 1982, long before the Irangate scandal burst forth on the world, the then Israeli ambassador to the United States, Moshe Arens, informed the press that Israel was providing arms to Iran "in coordination with the U.S. government." He did so in the hope of establishing relations with Iranian officers who would carry out a military coup, or who might be in a position of power in Iran during the post-Khomeini succession.[37] In this way, the Israelis, ever concerned about the outcome of the Iran-Iraq war, helped keep channels open to moderate or pragmatic elements in Iran, both among the clerics and the military, who might one day overthrow or inherit the power of the Shi'i leadership.

Yet too principled, too fanatical, often irrational, equally distrustful of the Zionist state, the Iranians just could not bring themselves to make a pact with another devil; with little material wherewithal to achieve their goals, they made enormous and, in the end, needless human sacrifices, without gaining much either for their ideology or for their revolution.

POSSIBLE RECONCILIATION WITH IRAQ?

The Game has now come full circle. Iraq was recognized as the aggressive state after its takeover of Kuwait in 1990. A year prior to that, Khomeini had died. Iran had tilted significantly toward the Soviet Union, signing treaties in Moscow that provided for Soviet arms shipments.[38] After getting all the help he could from the United States and from his Arab friends—the Saudis and Kuwaitis—Saddam Hussein decided to invade Kuwait, overthrow the ruling family, and annex that state to Iraq.

Soon after the invasion, Iran joined the international community in condemning Iraq's occupation of Kuwait (even though there is no love lost between the two countries, since Kuwait supported Iraq against Iran during the war). Iran's Foreign Ministry called for a pullout and said that Iran would not tolerate any change in the political geography of the region.[39]

Nor did it take long for Hussein to approach Iran for help. Since the end of active hostilities between the two countries in the Iran-Iraq war, Iraq was forced to keep a large number of troops massed on its border with Iran in case of renewed conflict. Thus Hussein quickly agreed to all of Iran's conditions to end the war. What followed was an exchange of prisoners-of-war between the erstwhile belligerents (many of the Iranian prisoners had been incarcerated for nearly a decade and had grown to manhood within the prison camps); the return of two key border areas to Iran and a promise to abide by the 1975 Algiers agreement, which gave half of the Shatt-al-Arab waterway to the Iranians.[40] By thus ending the state of war between the two countries, Iraq was in a position to remove the tanks and troops stationed along the Iraq-Iran border and move them south.

Many analysts agreed that a hidden part of the agreement was designed to return to Iran over sixty thousand members of the Iranian *mujahedeen*, a violently anti-Khomeini faction. This was another agreement that looked like a betrayal. The return of the *mujahedeen* to Iran meant that the members would all be executed.[41] News reports appearing on October 22 indicated that Iraq, responding to an Iranian request, finally expelled members of the People's Mujahedeen of Iran (PMOI). Many of them had already fled to Europe. For its part, Baghdad requested Teheran to allow oil to be piped into Iran in order to circumvent the international blockade of Iraq.[42] Also, the war having ended, Iran was now free to purchase weapons on the world market.

Enter the United States. In a sudden twist of events, Iran was approached, through Turkey and Switzerland, by the U.S. State Department to help in the struggle against Iraq. In return, the United States could help Iran enter the World Bank and the International Monetary Fund, important sources of monies for the reconstruction of the Iranian economy. In mid-September 1990, U.S. negotiators at the Hague announced that an agreement was very close to being signed between Iran and the United States to return more than 400 million dollars in Iranian funds frozen in the United States since the overthrow of the shah.[43] The *Economist* later commented that "the threatened tilt towards Iraq might be designed merely to strengthen Iran's case for economic help from the European Community."[44] In fact, Britain and France had reestablished relations with Iran at the beginning of the new Gulf conflict. Iran thus found itself in a unique situation. It was being courted by both Iraq and the West and was free to condemn both. On September 8, Iran announced that it would respect the U.N. embargo (except for humanitarian aid), and many experts believed that Iran would keep its word.

Although the Iranian leadership denounced the invasion, it felt that a U.S. military buildup in the Gulf was unwarranted and unappreciated. The commander of the Revolutionary Guards, Mohsen Rezaei, unambiguously stated, "The United States was long waiting for an opportunity to tighten its hold on the Persian Gulf, the flow of oil in particular, and the Iraqi aggression has provided Washington the golden chance."[45]

This sentiment was echoed in the statements of Iran's religious leader, Ayatollah Ali Khamenei, upon his hearing of remarks by the U.S. secretary of state, James Baker. Briefly, Baker had announced that the troops already in the Gulf might have to "stay in the Gulf as part of a regional security structure to protect oil supplies, long after the Kuwait crisis was over."[46] Needless to say, Khamenei was outraged and, on September 12, announced that "anyone who fights America's aggression has engaged in a holy war in the cause of Allah, and anyone who is killed on that path is a martyr."[47] He also accused the United States of supporting Iraq during their war with Iran and making Hussein "arrogant enough to invade Kuwait."[48] This is not a unique perspective on the crisis. In late September, millions of Iranians took to the streets to protest U.S. forces in the Gulf. On the October 21 episode of *60 Minutes* in a piece entitled "Iran, Iraq and America," Mike Wallace went into Iran and interviewed people from all walks of life: from ordinary people on the streets to recently repatriated prisoners-of-war to university students; and all agreed that the Americans and Iraqis were both to blame for the crisis. Many felt that it was the Americans who were behind it all from the start.

The Iraqi foreign minister, Tariq Aziz, was sent to Iran to meet with Iranian officials on September 9. It was to be the first official visit between the two countries since the beginning of the Iran-Iraq war. Official diplomatic ties were resumed between the two countries on October 14, and embassies were reopened in each country. Soon afterwards, the *Teheran Times* reported that Iran might deliver food and medicine to Iraq. It was later reported that Iraq would ship 200,000 barrels of oil per day to Iran, thus freeing Iranian oil for sale (a rumor Iran quickly denied).[49] However, it is impossible for Iran to deny that it is in a very good position internationally and domestically.

Oil at $30 a barrel gives Iran an extra $5 billion a year, which Mr. Rafsanjani intends to use to buy off popular discontent. President Saddam Hussein of Iraq may not survive his invasion of Kuwait. How odd it would be if the invasion ensured the survival of his former enemy, Mr. Rafsanjani.[50]

These were prophetic words, as we shall see subsequently.

NOTES

1. Gamal Abdel Nasser, the great Egyptian, pan-Arab nationalist, waged two unsuccessful wars against Israel. He was the principal Arab leader who challenged the West when he nationalized the Suez Canal in 1956. Saladin was the Kurdish leader of the great Moslem armies who defeated the Christian infidels and preserved the Holy Land during the Crusades of the Middle Ages.

2. The Reza Shah period in Iran's history is far more controversial than that of his son, Mohammad Reza Shah. Both Western and Iranian studies are extremely poor, while Soviet writings have proven to be more objective in this particular case.

3. Reza Shah was basically illiterate and spent most of his time grooming an army, suppressing internal orders, and appropriating feudal estates.

4. For a full account of Teymourtash, see Miron Rezun, "Reza Shah's Court Minister: Teymourtash," *International Journal of Middle Eastern Studies* (Los Angeles), no. 12, (1980), 119–37. See also Miron Rezun, *The Soviet Union and Iran* (Amsterdam: Sijthoff Leiden, 1981), 500 pp. This book has been reissued by Westview Press, Boulder, Colorado, 1988.

5. Miron Rezun, *The Soviet Union and Iran*, 139–40.

6. Ibid. See the last chapter in this book. See also Miron Rezun, *The Iranian Crisis of 1941* (Vienna/Cologne: Böhlau Verlag, 1982).

7. The forerunner of the Baghdad Pact was the Saadabad Pact of 1937, in which the Arabs were not represented at all, though at the time Iraq (Mesopotamia) was a British protectorate.

8. Fred Halliday, *Iran, Dictatorship and Development* (Middlesex, England: Penguin Books, 1979), 279.

9. Milan Hauner, "The USSR and the Indo-Persian Corridor," *Problems of Communism*, 36, no. 1 (January-February 1987), 29–30.

10. Iran sent more than thirty Chinook helicopter gunships to the Pakistani armed forces, including logistic support.

11. Fred Halliday, *Iran, Dictatorship, and Development*, 269.

12. Hamid Alger (trans.), *Constitution of the Islamic Republic of Iran* (Berkeley, Calif.: Mizan Press 1980), 31.

13. W. G. Millward, "The Principles of Foreign Policy and the Vision of World Order Expounded by Imam Khomeini and the Islamic Republic of Iran," *The Iranian Revolution and the Islamic Republic*, ed. Nikki R. Keddie and Eric Hooglund (Washington, D.C.: Yale University Press, 1982), 189.

14. R. K. Ramazani, "Khomeini's Islam in Iran's Foreign Policy," in *Islam in Foreign Policy*, ed. K. Dawisha (New York: Cambridge University Press, 1983), 21.

15. *Iran Voice*, September 3, 1979, p. 1.

16. *Time*, August 17, 1987.

17. CENTCOM is considered to be on a par with NATO in Europe and with CINPAC (Commander in Chief, Pacific Fleet, American Alliance) in the Pacific. It can land an intervention force of 300,000 troops in Southwest Asia, 450,000 by the end of 1990.

18. At one time Menachem Begin of Israel was actually supplying arms to the Iranian Revolutionary Guards in the Bekaa Valley of Lebanon.

19. FBIS: South Asia, June 11, 1986. Cited by Gary Sick, "Iran's Quest for Superpower Status," *Foreign Affairs*, vol. 65, no. 4 (Spring 1987), 704.

20. Ibid., 713.

21. U.N. Security Council Resolution 598 adopted on July 20, 1987, called for a cease-fire, exchange of prisoners and withdrawal of belligerents' forces to prewar boundaries.

22. See Milan Hauner, "The USSR and the Indo-Persian Corridor," 30.

23. See Lawrence Lifschultz, *Commentary*, no. 3, 1982. "From the U-2 to the P-3 . . . "

24. *Christian Science Monitor*, July 8, 1988.

25. *Time*, January 11, 1988.

26. The GCC had broken with Egypt when Cairo and Tel-Aviv made peace in 1979. Only Oman maintained its links with Egypt.

27. *Time*, January 11, 1988.

28. *Christian Science Monitor*, July 8, 1982.

29. *Los Angeles Time*, July 7, 1988.

30. Ibid.

31. Ibid.

32. *New York Times*, July 5, 1988.

33. *New York Times*, July 7, 1988.

34. *San Francisco Chronicle*, July 8, 1988.

35. Ibid.

36. Canada's ambassador to Iran in 1980, Ken Taylor, had helped several U.S. embassy officials escape the country. Iran thereafter broke off diplomatic relations with Canada and demanded an apology for the act. In 1988 the request for an apology was dropped.

37. For an interesting discussion of clandestine Israeli and U.S. activities in Iran, see Noam Chomsky, *The Culture of Terrorism*, (Montreal/New York: Black Rose Books, 1988), ch. 8.

38. See Miron Rezun, *Post-Khomeini Iran and the New Gulf War*. CQRI monograph, Laval University, Quebec City, 1991.

39. *Globe and Mail*, August 10, 1990, p. A6.

40. *Globe and Mail*, August 16, 1990, p. A1.

41. Ibid.

42. *Globe and Mail*, October 22, 1990, p. A7.

43. *Newsweek*, September 17, 1990, p. 6.

44. *Economist*, September 15, 1990, p. 50.

45. *Globe and Mail*, August 10, 1990, p. A6.

46. *Economist*, September 15, 1990, p. 50.

47. *Time*, September 24, 1990, p. 17. Ironically, Hussein has also called for a holy war against Western forces in the Gulf.

48. Ibid.

49. *Time*, September 24, 1990, p. 17.

50. *Economist*, October 13, 1990, p. 44.

5

Central Asia and Azerbaijan: A Blueprint for Civil War?

With the formation of the Soviet state in 1922, the Marxists who were in power claimed to have solved the so-called national question by creating a state based on justice and a recognition of the requirements of each of the country's numerous ethnic groups. This principle has been enshrined in every constitution drawn up in the Union until now. As the new regime's chief specialist on minorities, Joseph Stalin created the facade of ethnic harmony. The Communist Party boasted loud and clear that it had eliminated ethnicity as a source of conflict in a multinational empire created by the imperialistic tsars. In the years that followed, the USSR rationally presented itself as a model for multinational society. Under Stalin there were to be strict limits on what could be discussed in connection with this issue. The assumption was that Soviet society was henceforth immune to the ethnic conflicts and nationalistic insurgency movements so characteristic of most nations; as a result, by following the Soviet example other nations could enjoy the ethnic harmony attributed to the USSR.

As Mikhail Gorbachev's programs of *glasnost* and *perestroika* accelerated the pace of change in the Soviet Union, the nation experienced a dramatic and violent onslaught of ethnic conflict. Accordingly, the public record of national unrest in the Soviet Union has shattered the once sacred dogma about progress in the creation of a "new soviet man" (*Sovietskii Chelovek*) motivated by the tenets of Marxism-Leninism and immune to old prejudices and nationalistic tendencies. The progress in creating this "new man," the embodiment of a "Soviet people" (a kind of Soviet nationalism—*sliyanie Narodov*) has given way under the current political reforms to ethnic strife that is tearing apart the whole fabric of Soviet federalism. This phenomenon is exhibited in three distinct patterns: interethnic conflict, nationalistic separatist movements, and Russian nationalism.

Interethnic disturbances are an outgrowth of nationalist, separatist movements, which, in turn, are an outgrowth of grievances against the central Moscow authorities, whether they be Soviet or Russian. An outgrowth of secessionist motivations results inevitably in the rise of Russian ethnic nationalism. The most notable moves for independence have been in the Baltic republics, in Armenia, Georgia, and Azerbaijan. As an expression of discontent, demands for secession have received considerable attention in Moscow as well as in Western capitals interested in Soviet developments. Changes in Gorbachev's once hard-line stand against secession—in particular, his adoption of a position that simply requires a more cautious, orderly process of withdrawal from the Union—are evidence of the strength of this expression of ethnic unrest.

There are approximately 60 million Moslems in the USSR. They have been reproducing at a faster pace than the Slavic and Baltic populations; and if the present rate of increase continues, there should be at least 25 percent more Moslems in the entire Soviet population by the end of this century. By that time will the Central Asian Moslems still want to be a part of the federated union? Will they, like the Balts, wish to secede from the USSR, or would they prefer to form their own federation? Would they not accept to be a part of a new, Soviet confederation? Or is it more likely that they would fragment into separate states? And should the Soviet Union really be concerned over the future political reliability of its Moslem population? Five Moslem republics lie at the southern periphery of the USSR, and it must be emphasized that as Moslems they are generally neither unaware nor immune to developments in the Middle East or elsewhere in the Moslem world.

Here in the West, as with many other things Soviet, opinions and analyses of Soviet Islam are divided—perhaps more so in this case because of the very remoteness of the area and partly, too, because of the inability of most Western scholars to read and converse in the native languages of these peoples. A knowledge of Russian does not seem to be sufficient to understand the multifaceted problems peculiar to these nations. One wonders whether it is even correct to refer to them as Islamic, not because of the diversity within Islam itself, but owing to their ethnic and linguistic differences. Then again, one must see them as a collective entity, for they are not only Moslem (believers or nonbelievers); they are also, above all, Central Asians, living in one part of the Soviet Union that still wishes to be encapsulated in a federated union.

The ties between the Russians and the Asian Moslems are not inextricably linked; neither is there a separateness or a complete dichotomy of views and outlooks. For nearly two hundred and fifty years the Russians lived under a Mongol-Tatar yoke; one cannot help but notice in the Moscow metro the ubiquity of the slightly slant-eyed, high-cheekboned, ruddy-blond Slavic Russian. For more than two hundred and fifty years there was much intermarriage, except in northern Russian areas like Novgorod. When Tsar Ivan, the notoriously volatile Ivan the Terrible, then broke that Tatar domination with his capture of Kazan, he "took" a Moslem woman as his second wife. He murdered this wife just like he murdered his son, in a fit of rage. It was under Ivan that the Russian Empire began its slow conquest of Moslem lands in 1552. Before their decline and conquest, these territories had been the most resplendent centers of learning and culture in an age when Russians, and all Slavs, were still backward. Central Asian civilization—both Turkic and Iranian—has left the legacies of a "Golden Horde," of Tamerlane, of Persian poets and bards and the inimitable architectural beauty of Khiva and Bukhara. Not long ago, Samarkand celebrated the three-thousandth anniversary since its foundation. Modern Tashkent, destroyed in the 1960s by an earthquake, today a bustling, tree-lined metropolis, is— to be exact—at least two thousand years old. The melodious works of the Iranian poet Firdausi still reverberate in Bukhara. The Russian language is peppered with the exotic richness of Turkic Tatar. Every speaker of Russian knows the familiar words—*karaul* (guard), *kishlak* (village), *kinzhal* (dagger), *loshad'* (horse), and so on. In short, there is a blending of cultures that easily attests to the fact that the Russians had at one time been the mere vassals of the Central Asian khans.

On the other hand, there is such a marked difference between religions, races, customs, living standards, and philosophies that it is reasonable to assume that the majority of non-European, Soviet communities—the inhabitants of Transcaucasia and Transcaspia—have little affinity with either the Slavic population of the USSR or the Baltic nations (Latvia, Estonia, and Lithuania).

As for the contention that the Moslems reproduce at a faster rate than the Soviet European population—this may be best illustrated by data on the number of children born to women of different nationalities. The most prolific nationalities are Uzbek, Turkmen, Kirghiz, and Tadzhik (over three thousand births per one thousand women), followed by Kazakhs and Azerbaijanis. Nationalities with a less-than-average reproduction rate are the Russians, the Ukrainians, and the Balts. This is the reason why in the next twenty years the population growth of the country will completely shift from the European part of the country to the east. Already there are indications that by the year 2000 almost 25 percent of the conscripts for compulsory military service will be drawn from Central Asia.[1] These statistics have in themselves prompted Soviet and Western analysts to take a more serious look at the USSR and its Moslem peoples in the light of these demographic disporportions.

One theory has it that the Moslems will ultimately overwhelm the Slavs, that they will clamor for greater autonomy, more independence, and that they may one day even pose a threat to the Soviet (or future Russian) state.[2] Whether or not this argument is overstated is difficult to determine. It has seldom been repudiated since Hélène Carrère d'Encausse's and Alexandre Bennigsen's work on this theme, and until recently, few analysts have taken the opposite view. The whole argument really begs the question whether one can essentially speak of what the Soviets have defined as a "Soviet people." How seriously can one speak of a "standardization of culture" and of a merging of socialist values into a Soviet nation? Is the idea of a Soviet people a purely utopian, socialist ideal, or is there some truth in it all? Let us at least take a look at the record before Gorbachev came to power.

THE SOVIET VIEW BEFORE GORBACHEV

In the Brezhnev era, the view was the same as in Lenin's and Stalin's day. According to the laws of dialectics, there would be a merging *sliyanie* of the cultural identity of all nationalities into a new Soviet nation, which would qualitatively constitute a new entity. This new synthesis would evolve over several dialectical leaps, predicated on the full development and urbanization of the economy and the modernization of society as a whole. The bourgeois, feudal or semifeudal, features of the old order were supposed to slowly erode to the level of folklore. What this basically amounted to was a general and piecemeal modernization, or Westernization, of the Soviet Moslems. Westernization naturally involved Russification because Russian was the most advanced and consequently the dominant culture in the Soviet Union. This common identity with its Soviet (Russian) content contained five principal features. They were

1. a single, common territory
2. a single ideology and world view (Marxism-Leninism)
3. a unity of class and a high and growing degree of socioeconomic homogeneity
4. a common multiethnic culture, with common features of spiritual make-up and psychology
5. bilingualism and the increasing use of Russian as the language of interethnic communication[3]

On a superficial level these characteristics in no way contradicted Leninist and Stalinist nationality policy at its inception, that is, "nationalist in form and socialist in content." What both Lenin and Stalin implied by "nationalist" was primarily outward appearances relating to forms and symbols, the traditional arts, language, folklore, and literature. It was an attempt to blend local elements into a generally Russian, Soviet model, without necessarily substituting a Russian culture for the native one.[4] The natural bearer of this common identity was to be the modern national elite of the Moslem populations. Moreover, it was hoped that this would serve as a model of mature development, acting like a beacon, for the Moslem populations living south of the Soviet borders.

THE SOCIOECONOMIC SITUATION OF THE MOSLEMS IN THE POSTWAR PERIOD

Some have argued that Soviet power brought incalculable socioeconomic benefits to the peoples of this region. The British sociologist David Lane wrote that the standardization of culture is a worldwide phenomenon embracing all ethnic and minority groups. Lane concluded that "the cultural identity of the Soviet people shares some features with those of the mass cultures of the capitalist world: mass media, a premium on common consumption goods, wage labour, an urban environment and culture."[5] Perhaps Lane's argument in this respect is somewhat flawed in that it posits the idea of an urban culture that would be accessible to the Soviet Moslems. But it would be one they would find difficult to attain in the immediate future, given that that urban culture would draw them to levels characteristic of European and North American societies. Lane may be proven correct several years hence, perhaps at a time when increasing urbanization among the Soviet Moslems begins the development of mass cultures. What Lane is saying may very well apply to the urban elite in Central Asia, but that urban elite is far from being representative of the population as a whole. If increasing urbanization is on the rise (urbanization is synonymous with modernization), then this will surely have a mitigating influence on demographic trends, which according to Soviet statistics is still not the case.[6]

Survey studies have demonstrated that almost anywhere in the world birth rates run in inverse proportion to the degree of urbanization. We know that the Central Asian republics and Azerbaijan have large rural populations. The following statistics are noteworthy:[7]

Population

a) USSR	37% rural
b) Uzbekistan	58% rural
c) Kazakhstan	45% rural
d) Kirghizia	61% rural
e) Tadzhikistan	66% rural
f) Turkmenia	52% rural

It should also be borne in mind that most rural Central Asians do not speak Russian; they consequently cannot aspire to become part of an elite.

Urban culture in both Central Asia and Azerbaijan has always been associated with the Russian language. Until the 1970s, very few of the skilled
and managerial positions were occupied by men and women who were
not completely fluent in Russian. Today access to occupation and education
is greater than ever before. The Soviet State has vastly expanded educational facilities in Central Asia and for some time now has allowed instruction in the eight-year schools to be given in the native vernacular. To
bridge the gap between the quality of rural education (which is comparatively inferior) and urban education, Moscow issued a decree in 1971
allowing schools in Central Asia and the Caucasus to teach professional
and technical subjects in the native vernacular as well. This was designed
to foster social mobility and to increase the number of skilled professionals
who could not otherwise aspire to a higher stratum without the knowledge
of Russian.

Stanley Rothman and George Breslauer cogently argued that progress
and modernity are likely to be associated in the minds of the Moslems
with Soviet power.[8] By breaking down both racial and class discrimination
as criteria for upward mobility, the Soviet Union has thus been increasing
not only the ranks of the native intelligentsia but also their alienation from
the Russians.

In a remarkable study of Tadzhikistan, Teresa Rakowska-Harmstone argued that the new Tadzhik elite in effect was able to articulate the dormant
national aspirations. In connection with education, she wrote:

The introduction of a modern educational system and new occupational opportunities favoured the formation of a westernized native elite who acted as inter-
mediaries between the traditional masses and the Europeans.... The elite were in
a state of cultural ambivalence; their ambitions for power were frustrated by the
commanding positions enjoyed by the Europeans.[9]

This is an interesting point, and I shall come back to the status of the
Russians in Caucasia and Central Asia further on in this chapter.

Suffice it to say here that because of the progress made in the Moslem
areas of the USSR, the standard of living of Soviet Moslems is today much
higher than in the contiguous countries on the southern frontier, when
compared to Afghanistan, Iran, and even Turkey. But not all Western observers have agreed on this point. The population of the USSR adjacent to
much of the border speaks either a Turkic dialect or some form of Iranian
vernacular. They are either Sunni (Central Asia) or Shi'ites (Azerbaijan).
Notwithstanding this kinship, which is primarily religious, on every other
plane the Soviet Moslems have little, if anything, in common with their
coreligionists to the south. The neighboring states of Iran, Afghanistan, and
Pakistan, Lane argued, can be considered "authoritarian," and "barbaric,"
and they "have had little concern for the welfare of the masses." In par-

ticular, women, who take pride of place in Soviet Moslem society, are deprived of basic civil rights throughout the rest of the Islamic world.[10]

There has been much speculation that this may have been a consideration in Soviet decision making; it might have influenced Soviet policies in Iran and Afghanistan. Hélène Carrère d'Encausse is the leading expert in the field who in fact subscribes to this thesis. Other analysts have gone a bit further than that: Sovietologists Frederick Barghoorn, Zbigniew Brzezinski, and Rosemary Quested are of the opinion that Moscow had always coveted the Hindu Kush as a more proper southern boundary with Afghanistan than the Amu Darya (consider my arguments in Chapter 3). The British writer Malcolm Yapp even went so far as to say that in the event of the disintegration of Afghanistan, and of Iran, the Soviet Union might consider the incorporation (annexation) of these countries and "find some support for such a move through the ethnic claims of the Soviet Republics."[11] Certainly, this scenario had already been contemplated by the Soviet leadership in relation to Azerbaijan at the end of World War II.[12] But no evidence has been adduced thus far to substantiate this position, so it remains purely speculative. In fact, the late Alexandre Bennigsen wrote that "the Central Asian masses are ignorant of the world beyond the Soviet frontiers."[13] Bennigsen has been less consistent in his assertions. In the first study he made of Soviet Islam in 1965, he actually said that the communist Moslem elites would not be adverse to such an intervention, that they regarded it as their moral duty.[14] He emphasized the role of the Moslem elite, and three years after the appearance of d'Encausse's *l'Empire Eclaté* he agreed with her and said there might very well develop a strong "fundamentalist religious revival" in Central Asia that could one day advocate independence from the USSR.[15] Those who took issue with this stance seem to have been from the left-leaning spectrum—the British sociologist David Lane and the French journalist and contributor to the French communist newspaper *L'Humanité* Henri Alleg.[16]

The theme of religious revival in the Moslem republics is the next point of my investigation. Everyone has made allusions to it in one way or another. As a rule, Marxism holds any religion to be the opiate of the masses and the instrument of the ruling classes. Although the Soviet State and the Communist Party have been generally antagonistic to the Christian Church, had in effect destroyed the influence of Russian Orthodoxy as an established and autonomous institution (with the exception of Stalin's accommodation with the Church during the war years), there has always been a far greater toleration of Islam as an organized religion and far less anti-Islamic propaganda in the USSR. Soviet authorities acted in this way primarily because Islam was considered the religion of the underdeveloped masses. But the Moscow leaders also feared religious dissent, given that the Islamic faith was the religion of specific ethnic groups. They feared that Islam and politics for these people were one; if the Moslems acted politically, their actions would be an expression of a distinct cultural-political identity that may prove disruptive for the central power in Moscow. In other words, it was inconsistent with socialism.

The Soviet authorities accepted Islam with all its ceremonial symbolism and innocuous religious observances. They accepted Islamic ways as a way of life. Since Islam does not really require a church hierarchy, the task was made much easier in comparison to, say, the Christians and the Jews. There is a hint here that Judeo-Christian modes of behavior are markedly distinct from the Islamic. If one were to make a case for a "Soviet people," or some form of integrated *Homo sovieticus*—which would include the Moslems—then it should be safe to say that the Soviet Union is a melting pot of nations incorporating a common pattern of behavior, as Lane has in fact suggested. That notion would certainly involve widespread inter-marriage among Christians, Moslems, and Jews. Throughout the Brezhnev period, however, the statistics eloquently show that Moslems did not read-ily marry outside their religious faith. In fact, many refused to marry outside their Moslem community, even to Moslems in other communities. Of course, this could be imputed to the fact that because they have a larger rural population, the Moslems were more bound to tradition. Western scholars have all noted the definite cultural differences associated with religion that contributed to an unwillingness to be assimilated into the Russian nationality. (See the works of Richard Pipes, Hélène Carrère d'En-causse, Alexandre Bennigsen, and Teresa Rakowska-Harmstone.)

However, Soviet statistics also tell us that there has been a general increase in the number of Russian women who marry Moslem men. But what of the Moslem elites? Rakowska-Harmstone, writing in 1970, said, "Members of the modern Tadzhik elite hover uneasily on the borderline; outwardly they belong to the modernizers, but many are still believers and traditionalists at heart."[17]

This would seem to suggest that the elites merely paid lip service to the central power in order to maintain their local power base. This is an example of establishment or "official," secular Islam in the USSR. It saw no contradiction between communism and Islam. That is, virtually all Soviet Moslems more or less were expected to bury their dead, to marry in ac-cordance with Moslem tradition, and to circumcise their sons. But it was illegal to impose three of the five pillars of Islam: the *zakat*, or compulsory alms tax; the *hajj*, or pilgrimage to Mecca; and the fast of Ramadan. Other patterns of Moslem behavior that were not tolerated because they were not in keeping with established Marxism were arranged marriages, polyg-amy, the marriage of prepubescent daughters, and the dowry. These were considered rituals connected with a feudal past, with no basis in Islam.

D'Encausse presented a strong argument to bolster this view by stating that a "cultural identity," reinforced by religious faith, can and does grow in the Soviet Moslem areas into a political identity with its attendant political assertiveness. She maintained that the Moslems consider themselves as part of a community—the Ummah—and that simmering under the surface one easily detects a latent Moslem revival in the USSR. She strongly argued that even some outlawed "social mores" are practiced in defiance of Soviet law (e.g., infant marriages, the bride price, and private property). She saw only a temporary blending and harmony between Islam and Soviet communism and pointed to a kind of regenerated "*Homo Islamicus*" who would one day constitute a threat to the unity and fabric of Soviet society.[18]

Yapp, the British scholar, was of a different view. He likened Soviet Islam not to a resurgent, fundamentalist movement that we witnessed in Iran but to the Turkish example—secular and subdued, and above all relegated to the sphere of private life. He did not see evidence of any Moslem revival in towns like Baku, Alma Ata, Tashkent, and Dushanbe. Nor was there any evidence that the Moslems were seeking a return of the *Shariat* (Islamic law) in the USSR. He warned, however, that should the rate of urbanization accelerate, there could be a corresponding increase in religious revivalism. He, too, like Rakowska-Harmstone, was of the view that an Islamic revival, if it ever came, would be associated with urban groups and with an expected exodus to the towns. "In such a case," concluded Yapp, "the official Soviet Moslem hierarchy, an organization created primarily to impress non-Soviet Moslems, might become much more important, revealing itself as a ready-made leadership, capable of articulating Moslem grievances."[19]

Bennigsen forced an entirely new element into the debate. He introduced the subject of the Sufi Brotherhoods, a mystical sect known in the Soviet Union as Tarikat and the Nakshbandi, contending that these sects operated predominantly in the North Caucasus, in far away valleys and mountain fastnesses. He alleged that these religious orders had spread to Central Asia and particularly to the Republic of Kirghizia. The movement, according to Bennigsen, was essentially a rural one, but many urban intellectuals belonged to these Sufi orders. Naively, Bennigsen thought the Soviet secret police never infiltrated them.[20]

We must realize, however, that the Sufis of the North Caucasus, like the Moslems of that region, were few in number and were completely surrounded by non-Moslems. Also, these Sufi Brotherhoods had collaborated with the Germans during World War II; many were accordingly deported, and it is highly unlikely that throughout the Brezhnev era they were capable of escaping the watchful eye of so dreaded an organization as the KGB.

RUSSIFICATION

If we conclude that Soviet Moslems are cultural Moslems and that they do not derive political identity from that religious culture, can we then say that the present state of Russification will give them that political identity or political consciousness that will set them further apart from the Rus-

sians? Or can we say that the triad of urbanization/modernization/Russi-
fication—concepts that are synonymous—will foster some feeling of be-
longing to a Soviet people, to a unified Soviet nation?

To be sure, in keeping with its goals of achieving a synthesis of one
nation, the Soviet leadership promoted such things as intermarriage and
bilingualism. It equalized opportunities for education and social advance-
ment. Soviet leaders have tried nearly everything for fear of exacerbating
the ebullient ethnic tensions within the federation. But this was always
taking place in the context of an increasing Russianization, where the
Russian language, and Russian, or Slavic-stock, personnel, consistently
dominated. The influx of Russians (and of Ukrainians) into the Moslem
republics has aggravated these tensions and has alienated the indigenous
populations even further.

Some years ago, Columbia University's Edward Allworth came to the
conclusion that the prime objective of the Kremlin was to destroy the
national cultures systematically and to make these peoples as uniform as
possible. In a sense he was saying that the Moslems were running the risk
of losing their true identity. It is at first difficult to disagree with Allworth
and with all who are of the same view. However, when we are discussing
the problems of a federal state—be it Germany, Switzerland (the Swiss
Confederation), China, Canada, Nigeria, or India—we must somehow acknowledge that the culture of one particular group will always be more
developed than the others; to put it another way, one culture will tend to
be more mainstream than the rest—a situation that confers upon it some
measure of authority.[21] Although we should not underestimate the degree
of Russification, we should not disregard the influence this phenomenon
has had on the population in terms of general communication and modernization. That is to say, urban culture in the Asian republics is essentially
a bilingual one (one needs only to look at census and rural/urban language
statistics of the USSR). Bilingualism is less evident in the rural areas.

Most rural Central Asians simply do not speak Russian, or they speak it
badly, making it less likely for them to be absorbed into an urban culture.
According to some critics, increased social tension will most likely come
with the rise of urbanized, Russian-speaking Asian intellectuals who will
want to seek out their traditional cultural roots We shall come back to
this point later in the text to see whether this has been occurring on a
mass scale under Gorbachev. Other critics, like Lane, believe the impact
of urban culture makes itself felt in the villages "where the village intelligentsia, having had higher education in the town, in turn influences the
villagers."[22] This argument is fine, but it still does not prove that urbanization influences peasants to the degree where it forces them to assimilate
into the Russian nationality. If anything, urbanization only enhances their
upward mobility. By 1979 the proportion of families of mixed ethnic stock

in the USSR was 149 per thousand families; in the towns it was 181 per thousand families.[23]

The tendency to encourage the spread of the Russian language is a perfectly rational one; granted, it is a form of control over the other regions, but how else can so many different regions communicate with one another? In the other non-Russian regions, especially those that are far less developed, surely using Russian as *lingua franca* would be beneficial. This applies particularly to the Central Asian Moslems. The Irish in Britain, for example, have long since lost Gaelic to English, for the Irish were culturally and industrially less developed than the English. Consider also that all the Asiatic languages of the Soviet Union are written in the Cyrillic alphabet, making it far easier to learn Russian script. The Islamization of the Caucasus and Central Asia had brought these new converts—who were either Turkophone or Iranophone—the Arabic script, an alphabet never really congenial to the phonetics of the Turkish and Iranian vernacular. Arabic script fits in well with a consonantal pronunciation typical of Arabic or another semitic (like Hebrew or Aramaic) tongue. But Turkish and Iranian (or Farsi) are not semitic languages.

After the Russian Revolution, the Soviet government actually adopted the Latin alphabet for all the Moslems, following Kemal Ataturk's example in Turkey in 1928. Then, from 1939 onward, these Moslems began to write their national languages in Cyrillic characters, with minor modifications. It was part of the drive to stamp out illiteracy. By war's end, three-quarters of the entire population in Asia was able to read and write. Then too, there was the possibility of providing greater instruction in both Russian and the native languages at all levels of education. We must remember that roughly fifty-eight languages are printed in the USSR; it therefore proves cumbersome for an Uzbek to learn the works of a Tadzhik or for a Kazakh to understand Azeri. The Russian language thus serves as the language of communication between them. And it is solely through Russian that the more underdeveloped nations of Central Asia have been able to acquire any knowledge in science and technology from the advanced Western countries.[24]

These are the arguments advanced by a tiny school of thought to which I have always subscribed. And my view is that the assessment of any school of thought—whether a majority or minority—ought to be based on prolonged research and on the strength of data collected while visiting these regions for more than just pleasurable outings.

Another person who subscribes to these views is Henri Alleg. A Frenchman who writes in French, Alleg's obvious intention is to offer an apologia for the Soviet system and to respond to his own countrymen, to criticize scholars like d'Encausse and Bennigsen. His methods are similar to Lane's. He made a point of comparison against which the Moslems of the USSR could judge their current situation; we too are forced by comparison to judge and evaluate the situation objectively. For instance, Lane wrote that Russification was nothing less than a boon; he cited the example of India, where state organs and decision-making institutions use the English medium of communication, and where the disparate ethnic populations must communicate in English because their native tongues are not mutually intelligible. Yet, he asserts, no one ever decried the policy of Anglicization in India.[25]

The only weakness I find in Alleg is that he seems convinced that the Moslems are not necessarily united against the Russians, though he admits they have had their own focal points of tension. For example, the Turkomen and the Tajiks have always been apprehensive about the growth and dynamism of the largest ethnic group, the Uzbeks. Communication between them was always in Russian, and this seems to justify the large influx of Russians into Central Asia to maintain an organizational as well as a political foothold. Eighty, fifty, even thirty years ago, the presence of Russian as the only official language at all levels of the system served as a mechanism of control. This brings us to another point in the investigation—that of the participation by the Moslems in the USSR's political administration during Brezhnev's tenure of office.

POLITICAL REPRESENTATION

Opinions are as diverse as they are numerous in regard to the Moslems' participation in the political system. Right up to 1962, 75 percent of the members of the Politburo and Secretariat of the Party were primarily of Russian nationality, albeit the Russians made up only 54.6 percent of the population. By 1980, the Russians occupied 68 percent of the positions; Ukrainians 7 percent, Kazakhs, Azerbaijani (Azeri), Georgians, Uzbeks, and Latvians each 3.5 percent. The key posts in government at the all-Union level were manned by the Russians. One must assume, however, that the level of education of the Europeans was much higher, thereby allowing them earlier access to public office. This will also explain their greater numbers in taking up most of the public service positions at the republican and local levels.

In the last two decades, the Soviet regime has embarked on a program of massive ethnic recruitment with a view to running the affairs of state. Recruited of course were Russian-speaking, ethnic Moslems, who were perceived to be politically reliable, culturally modern, and socially more progressive than those who adhered to an ethnically homogeneous, traditional existence. In a sense, they were being co-opted into the system; they were thus expected to subordinate ethnic solidarities to larger obligations and duties as Soviet citizens.

This subject has not ceased to fascinate Soviet studies experts in the

West. Rasma Karklins and Bernard Lewis, Zbigniew Brzezinski and Samuel Huntington—and a host of others seemed to concur that below the all-Union, national level, 76 percent of the members of the Central Committee Bureau and the Republican Presidium of the Council of Ministers were increasingly co-opted from the indigenous nationalities. Only the Jews were seen as declining in political representation. Professor Michael Rywkin was the only one to actually compile data suggesting there might be an element of "reverse discrimination" in the Moslem republics, with non-Russians being given preference over Russians for certain positions. Affirmative action has also been reported in regard to women; they are apparently overrepresented in Asia as a sign of their equality. One must bear in mind that the population of these republics is extremely young, given the higher birth rates, and there are greater rural/urban and educational disparities. Before Gorbachev came on the scene, the policy was to recruit into both the Communist Party and the government bureaucracy nationalities in similar proportions as they were found in the population as a whole. In Central Asia, owing to the higher birth rate, that policy was aimed to strengthen the power of the local populations.

Precisely because of their higher birth rate, Soviet Moslems on the whole have been seeking greater opportunities for education, employment, and social mobility. There has been an increase in migration from the countryside to the city. This presents a considerable, but not insurmountable, obstacle for the Soviet regime. Until now the Central Asian republics have concentrated their efforts on producing cotton and agricultural produce (they are still at a relatively low level of industrialization); but having created a large intelligentsia, the elite would have to be employed in other, more industrialized republics, where it will have to vie for jobs with the indigenous population. This may be one of the reasons for "reverse discrimination" in the Moslem republics, resulting in Russians leaving for other areas. Then too, there is the problem of the division of resources: Some Central Asian elites in past years have been pressing for funds to diversify the economic base within their republics. This has led to mass purges and suppression—clearly an indication of how class conflict can sometimes be superimposed on ethnic conflict. Under these circumstances, it seems inevitable that campaigns against "bourgeois nationalism" have been a constant feature over the last two decades, with the local political elite as the main target. A high-ranking member of the Azerbaijani KGB, an Azeri named Gaidar Aliev, had, while still first secretary of the Republic of Azerbaijan, become notorious for suppressing the "anti-cotton" movement in his republic and for purging widespread government corruption in Baku.[26]

What this has meant for the central power is that it might become necessary for either industry to move into Central Asia or labor to move out of it. With problems in the division of labor and of resources, it was expected that the competition for jobs might prove to be that much more acute, with the Central Asians—if the theory of "reverse discrimination" was to be proven correct—reaping the benefits in the long run.

Enter Gorbachev

When Gorbachev came to power, the situation in Azerbaijan and Central Asia went from bad to worse. The nationalistic clamor for independence in the Baltic states reverberated across the Moslem borderlands. So did the Russian reaction to this. We must be mindful that *glasnost* and *perestroika* had from the beginning been reformist buzzwords from the center. Gorbachev himself has always been suspicious of Moslems and Moslem political movements. He never agreed with the Kremlin's intervention in Afghanistan. There is a Russian nationalist current that sees Soviet Moslems as irrational, corrupt, treacherous, and violent. To accommodate Russian nationalist feelings, Gorbachev has preferred keeping Russians in top positions at the center of the political hierarchy and the military. One of Gorbachev's earliest changes took place in 1986, when he replaced the Kazakh Communist Party first secretary, Dinmukhamed Kunaiev, with the ethnic Russian Gennadi Kolbin. Loud and violent demonstrations occurred in the Kazakh capital of Alma-Ata. Gorbachev was intent on purging the bureaucracies of Central Asia, especially in the Fergana Valley of Uzbekistan, and resorted to wholesale dismissals of party *apparatchiks*, accusing them of xenophobia, nationalism, corruption, and "tolerance for Islam."[27]

Gorbachev's first detailed statement on the nationalities question, however, came at the plenum of the Central Committee of the CPSU (Communist Party of the Soviet Union) on July 29, 1988. The statement was long on self-criticism about past relations between Moscow and the Central Asian republics and the cause of nationalist tensions and ethnic unrest. But it was short on proposals to solve the problem. He said that the years of neglect in the area of the Soviet Union's nationalities, the indifferently ineffective control on the part of the masses over the activity of leading personnel, and the active resistance to *perestroika* by corrupted groups who wanted to redirect national sentiments and aspirations to cover up the stagnation of the previous years were to blame for nationalist unrest in the Soviet Union. Gorbachev believed that the solution to the nationalities problem should be made easier when *perestroika* and *glasnost* laid bare these phenomena, creating conditions toward a democratic solution. That solution, Gorbachev argued, could be found by returning to the old Leninist norms and principles, to an "internationalist" ideology incompatible with any varieties of chauvinism and nationalism.

Initially, checking the growth of national sentiment and policing the ethnic unrest was the responsibility of the state (republican) governments. The republican authorities attempted to assimilate or co-opt the informal nationalist groups within the Party apparatus, thus uniting Party and non-Party political activists who were in support of *glasnost* and *perestroika*. In Kazakhstan, for example, the state leadership hoped that informal groups would prod the bureaucracies to address pressing agricultural, ecological, and cultural problems. This approach served the dual purpose of having the nationalist groups focus their organization and energies in a direction favored by the authorities without causing too many problems. But this assimilationist strategy was very weak and slowly fell apart as a result of the contradiction between democratic *glasnost* and the necessity of maintaining control over the growth of nationalist sentiment. Informal groups and religious organizations suddenly began to flourish under the impetus and spirit of *glasnost*. Criticism of the Republic's political, social, and economic problems, like any pent-up anger, struck a responsive chord in the whole population.

What Triggered the Soviet Moslems to Revolt?

Perhaps the best-known disturbance erupted over the issue of Nagorno-Karabakh in Azerbaijan. Friction had existed between the Armenians and Azeris since the early 1960s. The Armenians are resentful for the Azeris, since the latter are ethnically related to the Turks. Nagorno-Karabakh is an Armenian enclave lying within the borders of Soviet Azerbaijan in which Armenians constitute approximately 75 percent of the population. Armenia has often demanded the return of this area to Armenia, and Moscow has continually refused.

The troubles in this area can be traced back to 1936 when the Transcaucasian Federation joining the two republics broke up, leaving their territorial claims unresolved. The bad feelings between the two factions led to confrontations in the city of Sumgait and strikes in Yerevan, Armenia's capital. The earthquake that rocked Armenia in December 1988 did not diminish the nationalist fervor there. In August 1989, Azeris erected a barricade of the railway lines responsible for 85 percent of the goods bound for Armenia from the other Soviet republics.

Gorbachev quickly blamed Islamic fundamentalism for the violence, pointing an accusing finger at the Iranian Shi'ites. In January 1990, the Supreme Soviet voted to return all administrative control over this region to Azerbaijan. Yet the Armenian parliament responded by including Nagorno-Karabakh in its next Five-Year Economic plan. Activists of the newly created Azerbaijan Popular Front soon took to the streets of Baku, rioting, crippling communications, and dismantling the borders between the republic of Azerbaijan and Iran. The nationalist-minded Azeris of this area were seeking to join with their Azeri kinsmen in Iran to form a unified homeland. Apparently Khomeini's successor, Hashemi Rafsanjani, had fueled the rise of ethnic nationalism in Soviet Azerbaijan when he stopped off in Baku in June 1989 after a state visit to Moscow. He told large crowds in Baku that bilateral agreements he had just signed would lead to increased tourism and trade between the two Azerbaijani regions.[28]

On January 13, 1990, the rising crisis exploded violently when Azeris began to attack Armenians within Nagorno-Karabakh and in other areas of Azerbaijan. The approach of civil war hung heavy in the air when the first secretary of the Azerbaijani Communist Party solemnly declared war on Armenia. On January 17, a state of emergency was declared and Soviet troops were sent in to quell the violence. By the eighteenth, Soviet troops were ordered to protect civilians and to guard arms depots. On the twentieth, Soviet troops were called in to smash through the blockades that were set up by ethnic extremists in Baku; and as many as one thousand Azeris were reported killed in the fighting. Allegations arose that the Azeris had brought arms into the USSR from Iran to use in their bid for total independence from Moscow. Almost a third of the republic's Communist Party members burned their membership cards. Ekhtibar Mamedov, the Azerbaijani Popular Front's representative in Moscow, said, "If Gorbachev wants a second Afghanistan, he will get it in Azerbaijan."[29] By February 22, military cadets in Azerbaijan fired on Soviet troops, who were joined by their comrades from Georgia. Iran responded by issuing its regrets over the violence in Azerbaijan, and the Turkish government refused to interfere in the pro-Azeri demonstrations that took place in the major cities of Turkey.

There is an interesting irony in all this. On the one hand, the Teheran government condemned the intercommunal violence and acknowledged Moscow's right to keep order. On the other, it condemned the full-scale armed suppression of Moslems by the "Marxist sword of the Kremlin dwellers." The Iranians were only too happy to see Azeri nationalism quashed by Moscow so that it could not cross the border and threaten Iran's own fragile unity. It is ironic too that in the past, it was Soviet Azerbaijan that brought the ideas of Marxism to Iranian Azerbaijan and to the rest of Iran, while today the ideas of Azerbaijani Turkic nationalism are spreading quickly across the border to Iran. Both Iran and the USSR felt the destabilizing effect of Azeri nationalism. This may explain one of the many reasons why there has been so much constructive cooperation between Moscow and Teheran in the wake of Khomeini's death.[30]

The struggle between Turk and Armenian goes further back than the current squabble between Soviet Armenians and Soviet Azeris. The direct cause is linked to a genocide perpetrated against the Armenian people in the year 1915, possibly extending into 1916 as well. There had been a brutal and calculated attempt to exterminate an entire population of men, women, and children in Turkey's eastern provinces, which was theoretically a part of Armenia. There were some firebrands in the Ottoman Empire; the reader will no doubt recall my discussion of the Basmachi. In Chapter 2 of this book, I made reference to the notorious Enver Pasha and Haji Sami. Now I would also include among these villains the Turkish minister of the interior, Talaat Pasha, a man who reasoned that the Christian Armenians ought to be destroyed because they sympathized with the Russians, their Christian cousins to the north, in World War I.

A United Nations Commission on Human Rights in 1973 called it "the first genocide of the 20th century." The Turkish government to this day denies the Turks committed the crime. Between 1.5 million and 2 million Armenians were ordered deported to the deserts of Syria. Some died on the way from the rigors of the long march; others collapsed from starvation, thirst, and exposure. Most were callously slaughtered or drowned by the Turkish soldiers. Surviving children were sold to the Kurds. Some accounts say that more than one million had disappeared; other accounts put the number at more than one and a half million. It was a tragic episode.

In 1920, a series of Ottoman documents were published by an Armenian who claimed he had obtained them from a Turkish official. These papers, a total of thirty-one ciphered telegrams, were sent by Talaat Pasha to local Turkish commanders, allegedly exhorting Turkish soldiers to "destroy completely all Armenians living in Turkey, until not a single one remains."

Under the Brest-Litovsk agreements of 1918, the Germans and Soviets agreed to create a free Armenian republic. It was supposed to be carved out of Soviet territory. Many Armenian survivors of the Turkish, Kurdish, and Azeri massacres went there to help set up a Democratic Republic of Armenia, which was later strongly supported by Britain and the Allied powers. The Armenian nationalist movement—the anti-Soviet Dashnaktsutiun—was born there. But the Soviet Red Army overran the whole region in 1921, proclaimed a Soviet Armenian Republic, and then signed a treaty with Kemalist Turkey setting out the current boundaries. I should perhaps point out that the European Parliament, an elected assembly of the twelve-member European Economic Community (EEC), barred Turkey from entry into the EEC unless it acknowledged that the massacres of 1915 had been an attempt at genocide. So far Turkey has refused to consider the issue, and still is not part of the EEC.

Although on a number of occasions Mikhail Gorbachev received Armenian delegations clamoring for territorial rights, there was very little he was able to do to propitiate the Armenians. He and other Kremlin leaders have been sympathetic to their cause, but it is unlikely Moscow would want to antagonize the Moslems. Nor would Moscow want to set a precedent by appeasing the Armenians and thus give vent to the nationalist and separatist movements of the other Soviet minorities, like the Estonians or the Latvians, not to mention the larger group of Ukrainians. Hence the problem of the Armenians, short of emigrating from the Soviet Union, is an insoluble one.

The politically aware Armenians in Azerbaijan and in Central Asia often

compare themselves to Jews elsewhere in the world. They are bright, re-
sourceful, and enterprising, and they are not liked because of their business
acumen. They have a voice abroad because they, like the Jews, have a
diaspora. However, since they are Christian, they sometimes engender a
great deal more sympathy in the West for their cause.

This does not stand them in good stead with the Azeris and Central
Asians, who regard themselves as Moslems and Turks. Pan-Turkism is
slowly generating an appeal for the Central Asian masses by striking home
the anti-Armenian slogans, referring to these Christians as corrupt usurers
who are out to exploit the righteous Moslems. In Central Asia there is a
general feeling of solidarity with the Azeris in their quarrel with the Armenians. This was illustrated in the anti-Armenian disturbances in Ash-
khabad and in Nebit-Dag in May 1989. Interestingly, however, by contrast,
the non-Turkic Tajiks have tended to show sympathy for the Armenians.

Nationalist groups in Central Asia (usually in the form of popular fronts)
seek a number of different solutions to popular problems. They would all
like to see their native languages become official state languages. For the
most part, this goal has been reached in several Central Asian republics,
including Uzbekistan and Tajikistan. These groups also want a return to
the Arabic script. They believe that "one of the Soviet leadership's reasons
for switching from the Arabic to the Latin and then to the Cyrillic script
for Central Asia was to break with a literary tradition that had had a strong
Islamic influence and with literary activity in other Islamic countries."[31]
Since most young people cannot read Arabic and are uneducated in their
own literary traditions, many universities and high schools have sought to
introduce courses to remedy the situation (though they make the distinction that they will not teach Islamic ideology along with these subjects).[32]
Also, many of these groups have sought to have the Koran translated into
their respective native tongues so that it is accessible to the average person.

National movements are also concerned with the issue of Central Asians
moving away from Central Asia in order to find work or "a better life."
They feel that they are losing most of their talented young people who
could help the region develop, and they are justifiably disconcerted with
this trend. They also resent the immigration of Russians and Ukrainians
into Central Asia, Slavs who take up the best jobs and the powerful government positions.[33] They are tired of being treated like children who must
be managed. They also seek to rectify the bureaucratic practices of the
republic's leadership, in particular the rehabilitation of writers and political
personalities condemned in the 1920s and 1930s. They want to fill in the
blank spots in their history while rectifying the distortions perpetrated
upon them.[34] These groups also want to end their economic domination
by Russia (i.e., the central government literally robs them of their natural
resources yet makes no major effort to develop the region), and they desire
a solution to some of the horrendous ecological problems that aggravate

the whole region and lower their living standard. A typical example of an ecological problem begging for a speedy solution is the drying up of the Aral Sea. The Aral Sea is shrinking, and the dust storms that have resulted carry the salts from the seabed, which contain the residue of fertilizers and pesticides used on cotton crops, into the water supply. These pollutants have caused physical and mental deformities in animals and humans.[35]

The national movement in Tajikistan is the only one in the region in which at least some of the intelligentsia are apparently definitely Islamic oriented, ostensibly because they are of Persian, rather than Turkic, stock.[36] Tajikistan has its own popular front called Rastokhez (Resurrection) led by Bagir Abdfuljaber. The Tajiks fear they will be absorbed into a Central Asian, Turkic-dominated population and hence risk losing their Iranian culture and language. Thus they have sought support from another Persian culture outside the USSR.[37] The bonds between the Tajiks, Iran, and Afghanistan are strengthening as a result of this tension.

Perhaps the most unnationalistic of all the Central Asian republics is Turkmenistan. Turkmenistan is more of a tribal confederation than nation. This nonnationalism has been explained by Annette Bohr as being the result of a low level of economic and social development. According to Bohr, most of the population is still rural; the republic itself is geographically severed from most political changes; there is no sizable and active intelligentsia; and the Turkmen officials are "almost fearful of *perestroika* and tend to quash any popular initiative in order to retain their fragile ability to govern."[38] Like much of Central Asia, Turkmenistan suffers from the distorted development of its economy. The Turkmens, like other Central Asians, have little industrial development and are forced to import their finished goods and export most of their raw materials from Russia.[39] They are thus justifiably upset at the Russians and seek to improve their economy. They also seek to reassess Turkmen history and have been involved in opening a number of new mosques and translating the Koran. Thus as their culture becomes more important, so too does Islam. Like many of their Central Asian brothers, the Turkmens have been involved in interethnic strife, mainly involving clashes in May 1989 with the Armenians in Turkmenistan.

Unlike the Turkmens, the Uzbeks seem to be the most nationalistic of all Central Asians. Yet unlike traditional Central Asian nationalists, the Uzbeks believe they should be leaders in the region because they are the largest indigenous nationality and their language and culture is the most identifiable with those of pre-Soviet Turkestan.[40]

The major nationalist group is the Uzbek Popular Front, which is called Birlik (meaning "Unity"), formerly led by Abdurrahim Pulatov. It seeks to further Uzbek national interests through various means. Birlik was split in February 1990, and the new splinter group became known as Erk (Independence). Like its name, Erk seeks independence for Uzbekistan within the framework of a renewed Soviet federation while criticizing Birlik for not taking advantage of the political opportunities created by *perestroika*.[41] Prominent members of Erk include Muhammad Salik and Erkin Wahidov, both prominent activists and poets.

Nationalism has played a very important role in the Central Asian identity. Although interethnic conflict has tainted the relations between the different republics, there have been some attempts at reconciliation. On June 22 and 23, 1990, the three most senior officers of each of the five republics met to agree to a regional alliance that could conceivably lead to the development of a unified and potentially very powerful political bloc within the USSR.[42] They signed an "Agreement on Economic, Scientific-Technical and Cultural Cooperation" that established equality between the five republics; it established twelve areas on which multilateral accords are to be negotiated (i.e., economic cooperation, health, education, etc.) and initiated a mechanism whereby goals are to be reached.[43] This agreement took effect on July 1, 1990. They also signed two other accords that give an indication of policies the new bloc is likely to pursue in the short term.[44]

With this agreement, the nationalities of Central Asia may come closer together and achieve peace. What this will mean is unclear. Possibly, they will unify into a cohesive political bloc and give Russia a run for its money in terms of sheer bulk of population. After all, if they can modernize their economy, they stand a good chance of becoming very powerful economically based on their oil wealth.

Which is more important, nationalism or religion? At present, it seems that as a result of interethnic infighting that religion cannot moderate, nationalism is a more potent force. Nationalism and religion together appear to the Western observer as a double-edged sword—but a blunted one: The alleged importance of Islam has in fact receded behind the banner of nationhood. If this Moslem area, which excludes Christian Armenia, Georgia, and Ossetia, were more developed economically, at least the poverty that is at the root of the internal fighting would cease. But this may be wishful thinking on my part. Two distinct factors seem to be holding this region together and keeping it inside the USSR: The Moslem's fear of other Moslems and the strong presence of Russian forces from the center that bolster the Soviet Union's southern and southwestern military districts. From a military standpoint, the Moscow center is likely to be less keen on losing these southern, Islamic satraps than it is in losing the Baltic coastline to the secessionist-minded Balts. "Interethnic strife in Central Asia . . . which pitted Muslim against Muslim," to conclude in the words of one of the more perceptive analysts, "has brought the region to the notice of the outside world in a way that press accounts of poverty, social and economic neglect, and environmental degradation failed to do."[45] Central Asia and Azerbaijan may thus become a tinderbox of violence in the future, if left to their own devices. This is the main reason why the populations of this region unanimously approve a new Union treaty and are reluctant to secede from the Soviet center.

NOTES

1. M. Feshbach and S. Rapawy, "Soviet Population and Manpower Trends and Policies," in Joint Economic Committee, U.S. Congress, *Soviet Economy in a New Perspective* (Washington, D.C., 1976), 148.

2. This is the gist of the argument of the French sovietologist Hélène Carrère d'Encausse in the book *L'Empire Eclaté* (Paris: Flammarion, 1978).

3. M. I. Kulichenko, *Rastsvet i Sblizhenie Natsii V SSSR* (The maturation and the in-gathering of the peoples of the USSR) (1981). L. M. Drobizheva, *Kukhovnaia Obshchnost' Narodov SSSR* (1981). In English, see Rusian O. Rasiak, "The Soviet People: Multiethnic Alternative or Ruse?" in *Ethnic Russians in the U.S.S.R.*, ed. Edward Allworth (New York: Pergamon Press, 1980), 161.

4. See Teresa Rakowska-Harmstone, *Russia and Nationalism in Central Asia: The Case of Tadzhikistan* (Baltimore: Johns Hopkins Press, 1970), 231–33.

5. David Lane, *State and Politics in the USSR* (London: Basil Blackwell, 1985) p. 226.

6. For population trends, see *Vestnik Statistiki* (Statistical survey) for 1982, 1983, 1984, 1985.

7. *Narkhoz*, V., 1980g (1981), 17.

8. Stanley Rothman and George Breslauer, *Soviet Politics and Society* (St. Paul: West Publishing Co., 1978), 143.

9. Rakowska-Harmstone, *Russia and Nationalism in Central Asia*, 270.

10. Ibid., 312.

11. Malcolm Yapp, "Soviet Relations with Countries of the Northern Tier," in *The Soviet Union in the Middle East*, ed. Adeed Dawisha and Karen Dawisha (London: Heinemann, 1982), 33.

12. Ibid.

13. Alexandre Bennigsen, "Soviet Muslims and the World of Islam," *Problems of Communism*, vol. 29, no. 2 (1980), 38–51.

14. Alexandre Bennigsen and C. Lemercier-Quelquejay. *Islam in the Soviet Union* (New York: Praeger Press, 1967).

15. Alexandre Bennigsen and Marie Broxup, *The Islamic Threat to the Soviet State* (New York: St. Martin's Press, 1983).

16. See Henri Alleg, *Etoile Rouge et Croissant Vert* (Paris: Temps Actuels, 1983).

17. Rakowska-Harmstone, *Russia and Nationalism in Central Asia*, 283.

18. D'Encausse, *L'Empire Eclaté*, 246.

19. Michael Yapps, "Contemporary Islamic Revival," *Asian Affairs* (1980), 178–95.

20. Alexandre Bennigsen, "Minorités musulmanes en URSS," *Projet* (Paris), no. 147, (1980), 839–44. Another unofficial Islamic movement, particularly in central and southern Tajikistan is Wahhabism—a Sunni fundamentalist movement that originated in Arabia but probably came to Central Asia from Islamic fundamentalists in Afghanistan.

21. I lived in Geneva, Switzerland for at least eight years, and, notwithstanding the sovereignty of each Swiss canton, the dominant culture was decidedly Germanic, or Swiss German. The Swiss Germans control the Swiss army and all the Swiss banks. The Swiss Germans have a larger population and are economically more developed; they also control the Swiss police, transport, and aviation.

22. Lane, *Soviet Politics and Society*, 223.

23. *Naselenie SSSR*, (The Population of the USSR) 1983, p. 98.

24. One does not, for instance, translate a book on microcircuitry in electronics from English into Azeri or Uzbek. The translation is made into Russian, and the Uzbek and Azeri will read the Russian text.

25. See Alleg, *Etoile Rouge et Croissant Vert*, 231.

26. Aliev had a seat on the Politburo under Brezhnev. He was himself so steeped in corruption, however, that Gorbachev dismissed him.

27. See Yaacov Ro'i, "The Islamic Influence on Nationalism in Soviet Central Asia," *Problems of Communism*, vol. 39, no. 4 (July-August 1990), 56.

28. *Time*, January 15, 1990, p. 30.

29. *Time*, February 5, 1990, p. 22.

30. For more details on this crisis from the Azeri point of view, see *Kavbureau-Daghlygh Karabagh-Staline*, Tome II. (Montreal: 1990). For an interesting discussion of the Azerbaijani Popular Front, see Mark Saroyan, "The 'Karabakh Syndrome' and Azerbaijani Politics," *Problems of Communism*, vol. 39, no. 5 (September-October 1990), 14–29.

31. Ro'i, "Islamic Influence" 56.

32. Ibid.

33. To that end, the Central Committee of the Uzbek Communist Party has adopted a set of restrictions on the hiring of labor from outside Uzbekistan in order to train native workers to take over some of the higher government and civilian jobs. See James Critchlow, "Uzbeks Demand Halt to Russian In-Migration," in Radio Liberty, *Report on the USSR* (Munich), March 2, 1990, p. 18.

34. Ibid., 57.

35. Shirin Akiner, "Uzbeks," in *The Nationalities Question in the Soviet Union*, ed. Graham Smith. (Essex: Longman Group, 1990), 221.

36. Ro'i, "Islamic Influence," 62.

37. Eden Naby, "Tajiks Reemphasize Iranian Heritage as Ethnic Pressures Mount in Central Asia," in Radio Liberty, *Report on the USSR* (Munich), February 16, 1990, p. 20.

38. Annette Bohr, "Turkmenistan under Perestroika: An Overview," in Radio Liberty, *Report on the USSR* (Munich), March 23, 1990, p. 21.

39. Ibid.

40. Ro'i, "Islamic Influence," 56.

41. Ibid., 58.

42. Paul Globe, "Central Asians Form Political Bloc," in Radio Liberty, *Report on the USSR* (Munich), July 13, 1990, p. 18.

43. Ibid.

44. Ibid., 19. These documents were entitled "A Declaration of the Leaders of the Republics of Central Asia and Kazakhstan" and "An Appeal to the Peoples of the Republics of Central Asia and Kazakhstan."

45. Bess Brown, *Radio Liberty Reports*, July 20, 1990.

6

The Rise and Fall of New Babylon

And so, the Game continues. In its westernmost theater, west of the vast Iranian plateau, in a region traditionally inhabited by Christian Armenians, Nestorians, Kurds, and Shi'i and Sunni Arabs stretches the Mesopotamian valley and the highlands of Kurdistan. Here we find the land of the two rivers—the Tigris and the Euphrates—a land immortalized ever since the patriarch Abraham left his native Ur and set out to found two of the greatest semitic civilizations for the scions of Isaac and Ishmael. Here stood the mighty and looming towers of Babylon and Nebuchadnezzar's hanging gardens of Semiramis. Here, at the confluence of the Tigris and Euphrates, a luxuriant flora sweeps like a verdant blanket across an indescribable earthly paradise. Since the dawn of human history, Babylonians, Sumerians, Assyrians, and Arabs flourished in Mesopotamia.

Like the stately Babylon of antiquity, Baghdad became the Arab capital of a region that one can only describe as the stuff of dreams. Freed from the Persian Sassannians by an Arab-Moslem army, Baghdad achieved unparalleled splendor under the Abbasid dynasty. From his seat at Baghdad, the Arab caliph Harun al-Rashid was able to boast that of all rulers only he could exchange envoys with Charlemagne of the Holy Roman Empire. His son, al-Ma'man—likened to Solomon, king of the Hebrews only a few centuries before—was remarkably prolific in his passion for science and letters. He founded one of the first exclusive schools of translation, where works of antiquity were translated into the artistic calligraphy of Arabic. What a pity that Hulagu, the wicked Tatar, would one day sack the city and destroy what remained of the originals. Baghdad under the Abbasids became the epicenter of medicine and astronomy, mathematics and engineering. Baghdad was, in a word, civilization itself. The first travelers from Europe marveled at the architecture, the gardens, the irrigation works, its weaving arabesques. And before long Europe was to discover another bewitching subtlety: the enthralling stories of Sinbad, and the cavernous riches of Ali Baba as narrated by the beautiful Sheherezade. In France, Antoine Galland was beside himself with pride when the first translation of *The Thousand and One Nights* finally came out for Europeans to read.

BAGHDAD, CAPITAL OF MODERN IRAQ

In Baghdad, a new Babylon emerged. But it was not the Babylon of old; it was, rather, a form of pan-Arabism containing some features of a "leader," or personality cult; Sunni Moslem supremacy; and the rule of a single party, the Ba'ath, in an Arab socialist republic stamped with the indelible mark of a half-secular, half-confessional mentality called *shu'ubiya*. The latter is a genuinely untranslatable word, compacted with several layers of meaning that it would be best to turn to Samir al-Khalil's rendition:

Pan-Arabists tend to agree that after the Islamic conquests Arabness could no longer be defined racially, or by reference to some "pure" ethnic stock....Ideologically, shu'ubism is best understood as an idea that had to be invented whenever Arabism or Arabness became a problem; it is the idea of the enemy from within, the insidious, ubiquitous agent of a hostile outside whose presence is needed to reassure believers of what it is they are supposed to have faith in....Just as history's Shu'ubi was not only a Persian, today's Shu'ubis in Iraq can be communists, minorities and Shi'ites.[1]

By his own admission, Samir al-Khalil fumbles a bit with this unwieldy definition and, in a footnote, tells us that he would rather turn to another Arab writer on the precise meaning of *shu'ubiya*—that writer is al-Fukaiki, who simply states, *"Shu'ubiya* is a word applied to every foreigner who hates Arabs, denies their glories and prefers others over them out of hatred and jealousy."[2]

Oddly enough, there is something distinctly Iraqi about this attitude. Saddam (which means "the steadfast one") constantly referred in his speeches to the past glories of Iraq, even to a time when Iraq did not exist, when the Arabs, as we know them, did not dwell here; he talks of Babylon, of the Abbasid heritage, and of the battle of Al-Qaddisiya, where the Arabs first defeated the Persians. Saddam called his war with Iran "Qadissiyat Saddam." He often made speeches like the following:

The glory of the Arabs stems from the glory of Iraq. Throughout history, whenever Iraq became mighty and flourished, so did the Arab nation. This is why we are striving to make Iraq mighty, formidable, able and developed, and why we shall spare nothing to improve welfare and to brighten the glory of Iraqis.[3]

THE DISINTEGRATION OF THE OTTOMAN EMPIRE

From the mid-sixteenth century, Iraq, Kurdistan, and Kuwait, not to mention the rest of the contemporary Middle East, belonged to the Ottoman Empire. The Kurds were part of Iraq's northern, Ottoman-administered unit while present-day Kuwait was then an administrative part of Iraq's southern province of Basra. In a sense, under Ottoman rule there really were no borders. For the tribes who wandered across these desert regions, the concept of state borders—a concept of European origin—had no real meaning: There was nothing ethnically or economically important here, except that both nomadic Bedouins and the settled people were ethnic Arabs. In the same century, however, European expansionism was in the ascendant. The whole Gulf, especially for the British, became a crucial strategic outpost en route to India.[4]

When the Ottoman Empire finally crumbled, the British took up its possessions, which included not only the whole of Mesopotamia but also the Kurdish tribal territory and the Arab Gulf shaykdoms. In April 1920, Britain received from the Conference of San Remo the mandate over Iraq, which it exercised until the Anglo-Iraqi Treaty of Alliance in 1930. That treaty eventually paved the way for Iraq's admission to the League of Nations in 1932. The Iraqi Kurds were never given their independence as promised by the 1920 Treaty of Sevres. Kuwait, however, remained under British control until 1961. The only reason Kuwait was not admitted to the United Nations until 1963 was because Iraq had laid claims to it and its admission was frequently vetoed by the USSR, which supported Iraq. In 1963 Iraq and Kuwait signed a bilateral agreement as two independent states. There is certainly an artificiality about all the borders of Southwest Asia. Indeed, it proved difficult to trace borders along tribal lines; otherwise, the Kurds would have had their own state by now. It can be argued fairly and cogently that the state of Israel (not biblical Israel, but *Eretz Yisrael*) is itself an artificial creation, augmented territorially over several decades by conquest. And despite its insistence on Arab unity, we must be mindful that the Arab League was conceived in 1945 not as a federative instrument but as interstate organization. This, then, is what pan-Arabism set out to change—the artificiality of the frontiers.

The regional powers began playing increasingly significant roles in their bid for regional hegemony in the Gulf. There are two principal areas of conflict here: the area inhabited by Iraqi Kurds in northern Iraq and Kuwait that was part of Iraq in Ottoman times, but that later, under the British, became an independent entity. The reader will note that these borders were demarcated far away in European chancelleries. So, whatever I say in the following pages, whatever evidence I marshal against Saddam Hussein's pan-Arabism, his brutal policies of intimidation and war, the reader will understand that what Saddam is doing is basically calculated to redress the colonial heritage of the Great Powers.

THE KURDS

Against the Backdrop of the Iran-Iraq Conflict

Straddling Turkey, Iraq, and Iran, in the mountain ranges where the borders of the three countries meet, the Kurds are no strangers to the ups and downs of regional and international balance-of-power games. The modern history of the Kurds is commonly traced to the sixteenth-century encounters between the Ottomans and the Iranians seeking to define the political topography of the region in which the Kurds lived. The Kurds, in turn, became adept at manipulating the balance of power between these two empires.[5]

The confrontation between Sunni Ottomans and Shi'i Iranians was more than a contention over territory. It was also a confessional strife, and so far as the Kurds were concerned, the Ottomans had the edge over the Iranians, since most Kurds were (and still are) Sunnis. That, despite the fact that the Kurds were ethnically and linguistically closer to the Iranians.[6] This intense rivalry between the Iranians and Turks was mostly played out in Iraq, for Iraq was viewed as something of a buffer zone.[7] Just as the regional powers became adept at manipulating the Great Powers, the Kurds soon learned they could play off the regional powers against one another. Stephen Pelletiere cites the instance of the Kurdish Baban family who, around the turn of the nineteenth century, controlled "most of present-day Iraqi Kurdistan."[8] In the early 1800s, the Ottoman governor of Baghdad sought to bring the Babans under his control, though Abdurrahman, a Baban chieftain, was "constantly intriguing with and against the governor in Baghdad and the Iranians across the frontier."[9] In 1808, he was asked to relinquish his title over the *pashalik* of Sulaymaniya. The Ottomans acted on the principle that power should not be vested with a particular individual for too long. When the shah decided to enlist Iranian help, he asked for his reinstatement, knowing that refusal would give the Iranians an excuse to invade.[10] In the subsequent skirmish, the Ottomans were overcome, and Abdurrahman regained control of Sulaymaniya. Thus the Iranians increasingly came to dominate the area, and an Iranian garrison remained in Sulaymaniya until 1834. The Baban episode is a telling example of the pattern of relations that developed between the Kurds and the regional powers over the centuries. A similar instance can be seen in the case of Daud Pasha, the semi-autonomous governor of Baghdad in the early nineteenth century. Daud had decided to centralize authority in the province. The Kurds, particularly the Babans of Sulaymaniya, promptly allied themselves with the Iranians in order to resist Daud. In his attempt to break up this combination, Daud was defeated in 1821; this led to a decision by Daud to retaliate against Iranians living in Iraq, resulting in the Ottoman-Persian war of 1821–1823. Assisted by the Kurds, the Iranian army penetrated as far as Bitlis in eastern Anatolia. Although militarily successful, the Iranians had somehow contracted cholera and their forces were subsequently decimated—they were thus forced to accede to the Treaty of Erzurum (March 1823), which left Iraq in Ottoman hands.

These two instances reinforce the thesis that in the East old rules still apply and are often good guides for what happens in the region.[11] In both instances finding themselves in contention with the Ottoman authorities, the Kurdish chieftains resorted to Iranian help, which was readily forthcoming. However, the Kurds were also brought to the realization that dealing with the enemy of your enemy sometimes has its downside as well.

During World War I, the Kurds fought the tsarist Russian armies that had penetrated as far south as Rawanduz in the province of Mosul. After that war, the Treaty of Sèvres (1920) was concluded between the Ottoman government and the Allied powers; it was the first such document that contained articles relating to the Kurds. Article 64 laid out specific conditions for the establishment of a Kurdish state "in that part of Kurdistan which has hitherto been included in the Mosul vilayet."[12] The Treaty of Sèvres, however, was never ratified. By the time the Lausanne Treaty was being negotiated (1922–1923), the British apparently changed their minds. It all depended on the good will of a powerful foreign state. The British wanted to annex the Mosul vilayet to the newly created state of Iraq. They were able to impress this view on the other powers after a rather lengthy referendum conducted under the auspices of the League of Nations. During the interregnum (1919–1922) the British appointed Mahmud Barzinji as provisional governor of the Mosul province. But the arrangement soon fell apart, and the British were compelled to bring colonial troops all the way from India to Iraq so that they could keep the oil-rich province of Mosul firmly under their control and within the state of Iraq.

From Saadabad to Baghdad

In 1937, the Turkish, Iraqi, Iranian, and Afghan governments signed the Saadabad Pact. Certain provisions of the pact had clearly been crafted with the Kurds in mind. Referring to the Saadabad and Baghdad pacts (1955), J. M. Abdulghani argues, "Implicit in the two pacts was an understanding that Iraq, Iran and Turkey would co-operate in suppressing any Kurdish nationalist movement intent on altering the political status quo in the region."[13]

In the years preceding and following the Saadabad Pact, considerable

Kurdish insurgent activity took place in Iraq. A British-installed monarchy, under the Hachemite King Faisal, had been ruling the country since 1921; when the British mandate ended in 1930, the whole question of Kurdish autonomy came up again. Several insurgencies took place during the 1930s: one led by Shaikh Mahmud in Sulaymaniya and another by Ahmad Barzani, near the Turkish frontier. It was during this period that the Barzanis emerged as a Kurdish fighting force. The Barzanis were essentially a tribe, numbering, by some estimates, as many as eighteen hundred families, or nine thousand people. In 1943, under Mulla Mustafa (Ahmad's younger brother), they revolted against Baghdad. In August 1945 a major confrontation took place between the Barzanis with a force of four thousand to five thousand strong and an Iraqi army of approximately thirty thousand soldiers. Having been reinforced by some Kurdish tribes who were hostile to the Barzanis, the Iraqi units forced Mulla Mustafa to retreat. In September 1945, his entire clan crossed into Iran and made its way to Mahabad. There, in January 1946, was created the Mahabad Republic, a Kurdish separatist state; it was supported by the Soviet Union, which was continuing its occupation of the northern half of Iran since 1941. Mulla Mustafa was promptly made a general in the Mahabad Peoples' Army. It is interesting that the Soviet Stalinist authorities did not perceive Barzani and his Kurds as mere bandits, or *basmachi*, as they would no doubt have called them if Barzani's insurgency had taken place in Soviet Central Asia, rather than Iraq or Iran.

However, in 1946, when the Soviets withdrew from northern Iran, they abandoned both Iranian Azerbaijan and the Autonomous Republic of Mahabad.[14] As the Iranians took these territories back again, Barzani simply refused to surrender and crossed over to Iraq. He and a score of his clansmen trekked through Iraq and Turkey and Iran, finally making their way to the safety of the Soviet Union, where they stayed until 1958, the year of the Iraqi Revolution under General Qassem.

Revolutionary Times in Iraq

When Mulla Mustafa returned to Baghdad after the 1958 revolution, he was initially received very warmly by General Qassem, who hoped to use the Kurds against promonarchist tribal leaders, Arab nationalists, and Ba'ath supporters. As a Kurd, Barzani was accorded special treatment; he was provided with a mansion in Baghdad and a limousine, but he was barred from returning to his native Barzan, close to the Turkish border. Tensions did not take long to surface, however, when Barzani, who had assumed the presidency of the Kurdish Democratic Party (KDP), submitted a number of demands that among other things provided for Kurdish to become the first official language in the autonomous Kurdish region.

In the meantime, a conjunction of interests had developed between the Kurds and the communists. Both opposed Arab nationalism and the pro-

posed Iraqi union with Syria and Nasser's Egypt. The Kurds naturally grav-
itated toward the communists for two other reasons: First, there was a
fundamental incompatibility between the Kurds and the whole Arab left,
which was essentially Arab nationalist;[15] and second, the Kurds of Iraq were
drawn to their Kurdish brethren in the USSR who spoke and wrote their
language in absolute freedom. The Kurdish-communist partnership thus
came into full view during the Mosul-Kirkuk incidents of 1959 that resulted
in the massacres of Turkomans and members of the upper class in these
two cities. Starting as an Arab nationalist revolt at the Mosul army garrison,
the incidents unleashed deep-seated ethnic antagonisms between the
Kurds and the Turkomans.

But all was not sweetness among the Kurds either. Longstanding rivalries
among the Kurdish tribes intensified since Barzani's arrival in 1958. Edmund
Ghareeb notes that the alliance between Barzani and the communists, as
well as the government's harsh action against the landowners, frightened
the chiefs of the other Kurdish tribes, especially the Bardosts.[16] Barzani
was intent on settling old scores with the Zibaris, Surchis, and Herkis—
who all profited from his tribe's distress during the years of exile.[17] When
Lolanis and the Pishdar tribe, for instance, fled to Turkey and Iran, the
Barzanis simply appropriated their lands.

Meanwhile, relations between Qassem and Barzani deteriorated to the
point where the Iraqi air force bombed Barzan. Between September and
October 1961, the Iraqi planes reportedly razed to the ground 1,270 Kurdish
villages.[18] Qassem was also supplying the Zibaris, Herkis, and other Kurdish
tribes hostile to the Barzanis with arms and money.

The fighting continued off and on until a truce was declared in January
1963. Then in February, the Ba'ath coup took place. Lying low for a while
as the Ba'athists and communists settled old scores, the Kurds waited
patiently and then, in the spring of 1963, presented their demands for
autonomy to the new Ba'athist regime. Taken aback, the Ba'ath regime
unleashed its full fury on the Kurds by the end of June. To wit, a whole
Kurdish suburb in Kirkuk was bulldozed. With the advance of the Iraqi
army, the Kurds were forced once again to flee to Turkey and Iran. Turkey
and Iran were in fact closely involved in the situation, as was the Soviet
Union, which ended up protesting the decimation of the Iraqi communists
by the Ba'athists. The Soviets charged that the Ba'athists were put in power
by the CIA just as the shah was in Iran. A cease-fire took effect in January
1964. Another offensive was launched against the Kurds in May 1966; this
one turned out to be a disaster for the Iraqi government, leading to the
so-called twelve-point program.

Kurdish Factions, Iranian Support, and the Ba'ath

When the Ba'ath returned to power in July 1968, the party officially stated
that having some autonomous Kurdish rule was both realistic and justi-

fied.[19] There were compelling grounds why the Ba'athists should want to come to an accommodation with the Kurds: There were (1) growing tensions with Iran over the Shatt al-Arab, (2) an activist policy against Israel, (3) continued feuding with Ba'athist Syria, (4) growing opposition of the Iraqi Communist Party and other internal groups, and (5) a perpetual drain on the budget caused by the Kurdish campaign. The Ba'athists were consequently aware that the inability to resolve the Kurdish problem was a major cause for the collapse of their regime back in 1963. But there appeared no particular lull in the fighting, and by 1968 it finally resumed on a scale larger than ever before. Having received a new consignment of Soviet weapons in early 1969, the Ba'athists unleashed yet another offensive in the north, this time with sixty thousand men—"the greatest concentration of forces yet dispatched against the Kurds."[20] The Barzanis put up a fierce resistance and, though forced to retreat, managed to stall the Ba'athist advance.

Meanwhile, relations between Barzani and the KDP faction now led by Jalal Talabani and Ibrahim Ahmad had deteriorated. An intense rivalry had been developing within the KDP between Barzani, "the man of the tribes," and the reformist wing of the party led by town-bred intellectuals. The Talabani-Ahmad faction, also known as the KDP Politburo, had succeeded in forming close ties with the Ba'athists, whose radical socioeconomic platform they found reasonably palatable. The Ba'athists, for their part, preferred to deal with the Talabani-Ahmad faction, partly because it espoused a leftist platform not very different from their own, partly, too, because they were wary of Barzani's "suspicious links" to Iran and other foreign interests.[21]

The significance of these developments cannot be overstated. The Talabani-Ahmad faction was challenging the very basis of Barzani's tribal leadership, trying to extend its power base into the rural, mountainous areas controlled by Barzani while cooperating with the Ba'athists to undermine him. It was therefore not surprising that during the fighting in the spring of 1969, the Talabani forces were fighting alongside the Ba'athists, while Barzani was receiving arms and support from Iran. With the shah's backing, Barzani's forces had managed to grow in this period into a force of twenty thousand, well-equipped men, armed with anti-aircraft guns, long-range field guns, and antitank weapons.

From the military stalemate that followed there soon appeared, almost out of thin air, a major political document, the March Manifesto of 1970— a fifteen-point settlement that amounted to the granting of considerable local autonomy to the Kurds in northern Iraq. It was certainly a euphoric moment for the Kurds, and deservedly so. Kurdish was to become one of the two official languages; the festival of Nowruz (the Moslem New Year) was to be observed as a national holiday, and there were a host of administrative adjustments that largely satisfied many of the Kurds' original demands. It was an extraordinary turnabout.

The agreement, which came as a surprise to most, was widely acclaimed in the Arab world. In Turkey, however, there were reservations about its outcome. Within a few months, the number of Kurdish rebellions increased in Turkey. From July 1970 the Turkish government stepped up its vigilance in the eastern provinces. In April 1971, the Turkish government announced that a Kurdish independence movement in Turkey, set up and supplied by Barzani, had been uncovered. When asked about it, Barzani replied, "We are Iraqi Kurds operating in Iraq only. We have no relations with others."[22]

But the euphoria had been short-lived. Hailed as a watershed in Arab-Kurdish relations, the March Manifesto of 1970 did not produce a lasting settlement. Differences soon became apparent between the Ba'ath government and the KDP over the very definition of autonomy. Barzani's demand that Kirkuk be included in the Kurdish autonomous region was a source of major contention. The growing links between Barzani and Iran was cited by the Ba'athist autonomy plan. Al-Thawrah, the official organ of the Ba'ath Party, had evidence of massive flows of Iranian arms and equipment into the Kurdish region—for purposes of training the *peshmerga* at Iranian military academies and for joint operations linking the Kurds and Iranians against the Iraqi army.[23]

Barzani's increasing ties with the United States, and his readiness to receive military aid from whatever source, including Israel, were adding substance to Ba'athist concerns. These connections with foreign powers not only reinforced the Ba'athists' conviction that Barzani's ultimate objective was the dismemberment of Iraq but also precipitated a rift within the KDP that resulted in the defection of Barzani's eldest son, Ubaydullah, and other prominent figures in the party, to the Ba'athists. When asked to justify his links with Israel, Barzani reportedly said, "A drowning man stretches his hand out for everything!"[24]

Meanwhile, Iraq had signed a fifteen-year treaty of friendship with the Soviet Union (April 10, 1972). Coincidentally, as Soviet premier Aleksei Kosygin arrived in Baghdad to sign the treaty, U.S. president Richard Nixon stopped over in Teheran, where, it was said, the shah persuaded him to support the Kurdish rebellion against Iraq. What must have brought about a stronger U.S.-Iranian front, argues Pelletiere, was the report that the Iraqis were about to grant the Soviets port facilities at Basra, near the Shatt al-Arab. President Nixon, dismissing the objections of the CIA and overriding the U.S. State Department, ordered operations to commence in support of the Kurds.[25]

In March 1974, after having declared the autonomy plan as effective, the Ba'athists mounted an all-out drive against Barzani, committing "the largest force and the most sophisticated equipment ever."[26] A war of attrition followed and continued throughout April–June 1974. The Iraqi army was able to reach most of the forward outposts and scatter the Kurdish resistance, reoccupying towns like Ruwanduz. The fighting, pitting some sixty thousand Iraqi troops against twelve thousand *peshmerga*, was touted to be the fiercest since 1961. The extent of the cooperation between Iran and Barzani eventually reached the point where regular Iranian army troops, dressed up as Kurds, were sneaking into the fray by joining Barzani's forces; it was said that on several occasions long-range, heavy artillery was brought up to the Kurdish strongholds from within the Iranian borders. Iraq's attack were parried. The Iraqi force really managed only to bomb some Iranian border villages, scattering anti-shah leaflets in the process. At the end military observers agreed that owing largely to Iranian intervention, the Iraqis were prevented from destroying Barzani's forces during the December 1974–January 1975 campaign.

"The Great Betrayal" and the Aftermath of the Collapse

Every Machiavellian game of power and influence comes replete not only with surprises but treachery, betrayal, and ignominy. Such turned out to be the case with Iran and Iraq when these two countries suddenly decided to lay to rest their outstanding differences. Iraq was not a military match for Iran. The entente was initiated by Saddam Hussein, and, at least temporarily, it proved to be quite a coup for him.

On March 7, 1975, during an OPEC conference in Algiers, Iraq and Iran agreed at long last to conclude a deal over the heads of the Kurds. When it was announced officially, the agreement came as a surprise to everyone, not least to the Kurds themselves: The shah had decided to abandon his erstwhile allies, and almost overnight he was branded no less treacherous than the man with whom he was striking the deal. Within hours of the signing of the Algiers document, Iran began withdrawing its forces from Iraq and cutting off aid to Barzani. Taking advantage of the new development, the Iraqis mounted a major offensive against the Kurds, breaking through Ruwanduz Valley and threatening the Kurdish military headquarters in Haj Umran.

Stunned by the turn of events, Barzani proudly vowed to fight on. A few days later, however, after a brief meeting with the shah, Barzani announced he would not continue to fight. It had become pointless. Split on the issue, the KDP leadership also decided to give up. Barzani himself, along with his family, some close associates, and several thousand *peshmerga*, crossed the border into Iran. But he was already a very sick man; in 1976, he moved to the United States, where he underwent treatment for lung cancer. Three years later, in March 1979, he died, thus bringing a unique chapter in Kurdish history to a close.

When Mulla Mustafa Barzani passed from the scene, the KDP broke into several factions. One faction grew around Barzani's sons, Idris and Masoud, establishing the KDP Provisional Command (KDPPC). Another group, the Patriotic Union of Kurdistan (PUK), was the first to instigate guerrilla activities. Advocating Marxist principles and condemning the Barzani leadership as "reactionary," PUK was headed by Talabani and widely believed to be backed by Syria.

Consequently, KDPPC and PUK were soon on a collision course. In July 1976, PUK charged that Barzani supporters had killed several PUK men on Turkish territory. Clashes between the two sides continued near the Iraqi-Turkish border. In one incident, in the fall of 1978, two prominent PUK leaders were killed by men loyal to the Barzanis. With the advent of the Islamic Revolution in Iran, the Barzanis secured strong ties with the new regime. The leadership of the Kurdish Democratic Party supported the Khomeini regime against the Kurdish insurrection in Mahabad and Sanandaj in the immediate aftermath of the revolution. The eye-opening spectacle of the Barzani Kurds helping Shi'i fundamentalists quash fellow Sunni Kurds in neighboring Iran must have been bewildering, to say the least. But let us not forget for a single moment that Mulla Mustafa himself had been reluctant to offend the shah and, in his day, had renounced all connection with the Iranian Kurdish movement.[27] Thus Idris and Masoud could claim to be consistent with paternal tradition.

The Kurdish insurgency in Iran was eventually contained, but not until some serious skirmishing had taken place. In March 1980, the Iranian Kurds retook Sanandaj, and the central government responded by reducing the city to rubble in a fierce artillery barrage.[28] The Kurds, in turn, pulled back to the mountains and declared a liberated zone west of Lake Urumiya. Among the forces controlling the region was Abdurrahman Gassemlou's KDP of Iran (KDPI).

Three months later, in September 1980, Iraqi troops entered Iranian Khuzistan, and the Iran-Iraq war was on. By December of 1980, Iraqi forces entered Iranian Kurdistan, coming within fifty miles of Sanandaj. How ironic that the Iraqis, who had just brutally suppressed a Kurdish insurrection in their own country, were now supporting Iranian Kurds in their struggle against the Khomeini Islamic government.[29]

In the meantime, Talabani had set up headquarters in Damascus after the collapse of Barzani's rebellion and after war had erupted between Iran and Iraq. PUK proceeded to establish bases in the Sulaymaniya region of Iraq. In contrast to the Barzanis, Talabani decided to help the Iranian Kurds and even agreed to allow Iraqi army units to pass through the region under his control to deliver weapons to Ghassemlou. Thus, when Iran thrust into northern Iraq in the summer of 1983, with the Barzanis spearheading the drive, Talabani was faced with a crucial dilemma: Was he to ally himself with the Iranians, joining forces with the villainous Barzanis, something he would never have done before?

Taking advantage of Talabani's predicament, Saddam Hussein renewed his offer of limited autonomy in return for PUK support in defending northern Iraq against the Iranians. In January 1984, an exchange of prisoners was made between Talabani and Baghdad. PUK forces were henceforth incorporated into the regular Iraqi army as border guards. The war in the north had become a war of proxies, with both sides depending heavily on Kurdish surrogate forces—Iraq on Talabani and Ghassemlou, Iran on the Barzanis.[30] Once again, a balance-of-power game was being played, with the Kurds as both pawns and manipulators. The Saddam-Talabani arrangement was most discomforting to Turkey, however. Pelletiere thoughtfully observed that "with a Kurdish population of over 5 million in eastern Anatolia (adjacent to Iraqi Kurdistan) the Turks feared the effect of Iraq's offer of semi-autonomy to the Kurds."[31] Faced with an active Kurdish separatist movement on their territory, "the Turks," concluded Pelletiere, "could reasonably complain to both Iran and Iraq that by arming the Kurds, they risk destabilizing the whole Turkish-Iraq-Iran triangle."[32]

In December 1986, at the height of the Iran-Iraq war, a three-day conference was held in Teheran under the rallying motif "Cooperation Conference of Iraq People." The conference brought together diverse Iraqi groups whose only shared attribute was their opposition to the Ba'ath regime. One of the main objectives of the three-day conference was to bring together the two main factions of the Iraqi opposition and the Islamic movement. Many secular politicians also participated, including ex-monarchists, ex-Ba'athists, Christians, and distinguished Iraqi personalities.[33] Only the Iraqi communists did not show up. The conference was addressed by the Iranian president, Ali Khamenei, as well as Prime Minister Hossein Mousavi, the speaker of the Iranian parliament, Hashemi Rafsanjani, and Foreign Minister Ali Akbar Velayati. "President Khamenei confirmed Iran's commitment to an independent and free Iraq within its recognized international borders—a clear warning that Iran would not hesitate to challenge any intervention by other countries in the affairs of Iraq."[34] The message was obviously aimed at Turkey, a neighboring country and a member of NATO. A Turkish press correspondent noted:

There is no shortage of excuses for Turkey's possible intervention [in Iraq]. Turkey has had territorial claims to Mosul, Kirkuk and other northern cities of Iraq since 1932. But the League of Nations had ruled in Iraq's favour at that time. A minority of Turkomans still live in northern Iraq which may also become Turkey's "legitimate" excuse for its intervention.[35]

Turkey's historical claims to the Mousul-Kirkuk area had been the focus of persistent attention. Iqbal Asaria noted that Turkey has periodically expressed its claim to northern Iraq, an area that used to be the vilayet of Mosul under the Ottoman Empire.[36] He further argued that Turkey's dependence on the oil pipeline from Kirkuk, and the possible impact of any change on its large, but suppressed, Kurdish population, may be used as an excuse if and when both the United States and Turkey ever sought to dismember Iraq. At a time when the Gulf War was going well for Iran, the Khomeini leadership sent clear signals that it would not countenance any such move on the part of Turkey.[37] In a related theme, Zubaida Umar argued that Turkey had not done much to espouse the cause of the Turkomens in the Kirkuk area, estimated to be around one million. However, "as Saddam Hussein nears the end of his tether, the [Turks] might use them as a pretext for intervention,"[38] Umar added, writing at a moment when it was believed that the Iranians would capture Basra.

Such optimism notwithstanding, on August 14, 1986, Turkish air force planes attacked Kurdish sites along the Iraqi border following an incident in which Kurdish guerrillas ambushed Turkish soldiers. Baghdad radio said that 165 Kurdish guerrillas had died in the raids, but some sources put the figure as 200 or even higher. It was after this incident that frequent references to Turkey started appearing in the Iranian press. Under a headline, "Turkey Advised to Maintain Neutrality," the Iranian official newspaper, *Kayhan*, reported a Kurdish deputy in the Iranian Majlis, Mustafa Qaderi, as saying that "Turkey seems to be collaborating with the Iraqi regime and its mercenaries, despite claims of being neutral in the war." According to *Kayhan*, Qaderi (deputy for the Kurdish towns of Piranshahr and Sardasht) issued a warning that the "Turkish Government should not covet the Iraqi northeastern oil-rich province of Kirkuk," also noting that "Iraq's natural resources belong to the Moslem Iraqi nation."[39] The interesting spectacle of a Kurdish deputy sitting in the Iranian Majlis and making pointed references to Turkey's territorial ambitions in northern Iraq indicates how complicated the regional configuration was at the height of the eight-year war.

The Turkish point of view was given amply by Mehmet Osmanoglu, a Turkish journalist:

Looking at some realistic scenarios of the Iraqi future, then, Moslems have reasons to feel apprehensive about "the Turkish factor." . . . Should it become obvious that the Ba'thist regime in Baghdad cannot withstand the Iranian pressure and that it must fall, one must expect the Turkish army to occupy northern Iraq on the basis of "historical claims" that it once formed part of the Turkish Empire. . . . No doubt, this will be done with the full connivance of NATO and the USA. Given the fact that, politically speaking, Turkey has lost its Islamic moorings, such an outcome of the Iran-Iraq war will not be conducive to the emergence of a new Islamic order in the Muslim Middle East which is the ultimate goal of this struggle.[40]

One does not have to subscribe to this journalist's political logic to recognize the import of the ideological factor in the situation. As the Kurdish insurgency was being played out against the backdrop of the Iran-Iraq war,

a Turkish involvement in that conflict would no doubt have kindled the
ideological differences between Iran and Turkey, which were so skillfully
masked. When Osmanoglu spoke of a Turkey that had "lost its Islamic
moorings," or when he argued that "the expansion of the secularist Turkish
state in the Middle East will retard the process of Islamic self-assertion,"
his statements, whether accurate or not, highlighted the ideological in-
congruity between Shi'i fundamentalism and Kemalist Westernism.

But the Ba'athist regime in Baghdad did successfully withstand every
Iranian onslaught. Baghdad did not fall. Turkey did not and could not
occupy northern Iraq on the basis of the Ottoman Empire's "historical
claims." And it was wishful thinking to believe that the United States would
come to the assistance of the Turks. Indeed, as I explained in Chapter 4
(the exposition on Iran), the Americans came to the assistance of the Iraqis.
At the end of the Iran-Iraq war, Western think tanks and learned and
scholarly journals and academic conferences from around the world began
investigating the consequences of that war. Since more than half of Iraqi
citizens were Shi'ites, it was asked: Why had that Ba'ath regime not fallen
against Shi'i Iran? As Samir al-Khalil put it in his 1989 book, *Republic of
Fear*, "Why has Iraq's largely Shi'ite soldiery not defected, and why have
the Iraqi people as a whole remained willing to fight?" Was there really no
palpably tangible opposition to Saddam Hussein inside Iraq? The answer
was crystal clear. That opposition, or what was left of it, had either fled or
been destroyed—like Saddam's periodic purges of ambitious officers whom
he had always considered a threat to his supreme power. And what of the
Kurds, whose exploits against the regime have been the subject of this
narrative so far? Had they been completely written off in this cynical cycle
of cooperation and perfidy? Just about! That is, until the end of the next
Gulf War, when Saddam's Ba'ath regime was coming apart at the seams.

It was Saddam Hussein's last attack on the Iraqi Kurds—in addition to
his victories in the south—that ultimately precipitated the end to the Iran-
Iraq war. In the early spring of 1988, after a successful Iranian armored
thrust against Iraqi forces in the northern sector of the front, the Iraqis
retaliated—not against the Iranians, but against their own Iraqi Kurds living
in the town of Halabja. They launched an attack that claimed more than
five thousand innocent civilians. For the most part the victims were young
children and the elderly, completely unaware that Baghdad's air force
would drop poison gas on the town and remorselessly flout the convention
outlawing chemical warfare, an international treaty to which Iraq itself was
a party. This episode was given scant attention in the Western media; it
was treated as little better than a human-interest story at a time when the
West was too preoccupied with Israel's almost daily suppression of the
Palestinian Intifada (the uprising by Arab Palestinians in the Israeli-occupied West Bank and Gaza Strip).

Needless to say, the poison gas attack on the town of Halabja constitutes the single most enormous massacre of civilians in one place at one time since the Nazi atrocities. Yet Western commentators, especially before 1990, would often present Iraq's more moderate image, in contrast with a more deviant and treacherous Iran. There were, however, some dissenting voices in the United States. The most vocal of the criticisms came from the *New Republic*'s editor-in-chief, Martin Peretz. To be sure, he was one of the few exceptions to the stonelike silence. The style of the accusation was fulminating and sweeping. Writing in his magazine's "Cambridge Diarist" column, he explicitly stated:

The Kurds [are] a more ancient people with deeper attributes of nationhood than the most perfervid Palestinian tribunes could possibly claim for themselves.... It is a measure of the prevailing norms in Sunni Islam that these outrages have produced scarcely a shudder of discomfort from Iraq's allies, including most notably Saudi Arabia, Jordan, Egypt and the residual legatee of pan-Arabism, the PLO.[41]

In the same breath, Peretz reminded us how much perhaps Iraqi Shi'ites, the Kurds, and some Iranians owed to the former Israeli prime minister, Menachem Begin, for having destroyed Iraq's (Saddam Hussein's) nuclear reactor in 1981.[42]

THE CRISIS OVER KUWAIT

During the early morning hours of August 2, 1990, Iraqi tanks rumbled across the border of Kuwait and quickly put down any resistance. There was considerable international furor over the event. The United States reacted immediately. So did most of Europe and the Soviet Union. Saudi Arabia could not feel safe anymore. It was felt that there was not a single Arab power that could stand up to Saddam Hussein. The Iranians, as we know, were suddenly offered a peace treaty to neutralize them in regard to the new conflict in the Gulf. Let us look more closely at the background to the Kuwaiti-Iraqi dispute.

Iraq had in the past made a number of claims on Kuwait, its tiny neighbor to the south and ally in the war. After that war, Iraq had spoken out against Kuwait's overproduction of oil, an overproduction that drove down the price of oil and would cost Iraq much in the way of foreign exchange earnings (Iraq depends upon oil for 95 percent of its foreign exchange). Hussein not only believed that this was in direct violation of OPEC quotas, but it represented a danger to all Middle Eastern economies, his own especially. Hussein was also involved in a quarrel with Kuwait over the Rumaila oilfields. During the Iran-Iraq war, Hussein had accused Kuwait of moving the border between the two countries northward, so that Kuwait could pump oil from the Iraqi field. Thus, he sought approximately 2.4 billion dollars in compensation.[43] Furthermore, the Iraqi leader wanted

Kuwait to write off the 10–20 billion dollars worth of loans Kuwait had made to Iraq during the war. Since Iraq had been doing all the fighting, one can understand Saddam's insistence. Saddam also sought to seize Kuwait's Bubiyan Island in order to turn it into a port. It is to be noted that Iraq has long had the distinct disadvantage of having no sea port; Saddam obviously felt that the port was a strategic and economic asset. Another reason for the invasion was simply to appropriate for the growing Iraqi economy and military all of Kuwait's wealth. By controlling Kuwait, Iraq would hold 20 percent of the world's proven oil reserves. Perhaps by controlling Saudi Arabia, Iraq would be the world's major oil supplier and a power to be reckoned with in the world. Saddam must have realized his war against Iran was useless and unnecessary when compared to the annexation of the Arab oil shaykdoms.

Thus, on August 2 Iraq invaded, and on August 8 Kuwait was annexed to Baghdad. The immediate Western reaction was outrage. The United States was anxious not to let Hussein go any further and attack Saudi Arabia, the main U.S. ally in the region. Backing the Americans' fears, the whole world joined in condemning the actions of Iraq. The U.N. Security Council condemned the action by a fourteen to one margin and adopted Resolution 665, which placed trade sanctions on Iraq, implying that no member of the United Nations was to be allowed to trade with Iraq.

The United Nations approved the deployment of a security force to the Gulf to enforce its sanctions. An international coalition force from the United States, Britain, Canada, Belgium, Morocco, Spain, France, Egypt, the Netherlands, Syria, Bangladesh, Greece, Italy, Australia, and the GCC (as mentioned in Chapter 4, the Gulf Cooperation Council, an alliance made up of Saudi Arabia, Bahrain, Oman, the United Arab Emirates, and Qatar) was quickly organized in the Persian Gulf and in Saudi Arabia. In addition to this, important Western financial institutions froze all Iraqi and Kuwaiti assets so that Iraq could not draw upon its foreign holdings or those of its conquered neighbor.

Thousands of foreigners were trapped in Iraq and Kuwait. These "hostages" were either allowed to leave (as in the case of Egyptians, Turks, and nationals from Pakistan and Bangladesh) or denied exit (the Japanese, Soviets, Germans, French, Italians, Australians, and especially the Americans and British).[44] Soon afterwards, Baghdad announced that the "hostages" would be used as human shields at specific military installations in order to protect the installations. Initially, only women and children, the elderly, and the infirm from all these countries were allowed to leave. Those allowed to go, the Third World refugees, were permitted to cross over the Iraq border. Most went to Jordan and swelled the existing refugee camps subsisting on the meager supplies sent to the area by the world relief funds. Before Christmas most West Europeans were allowed to leave as a goodwill gesture.

WHY THE UNITED STATES OUGHT TO TAKE A SHARE OF THE BLAME

Surely the Americans themselves are to blame for the developments in the Gulf. I have come to the point in my narrative where I would like to invite the reader to make that choice. Reference has already been made in the chapter on Iran to the incoherence of U.S. policies. In the war against Iran, the Americans had helped Saddam Hussein with cryptic intelligence information; the United States Navy in the Gulf performed diversionary tactics, and there was some direct engagement against the Iranians in the Strait of Hormuz. There was the usual lobbying on Capitol Hill by pro-Arab, pro-Iraqi, anti-Zionist groups. Worst of all—for the conscience of academics is at stake here—is that there were pleas on behalf of Saddam by a number of misguided American and European intellectuals, not to mention pro-Iraqi commercial interests in the United States.

Since the Iran-Iraq war, Iraq had been closely tied to the West economically. Baghdad had received large numbers of weapons from the West and the Soviet Union; moreover, the Iraqis had established good relations with all the Gulf shaykdoms—all conservative ruling families. Some were prepared to give Saddam the benefit of the doubt. Others said he had turned over a new leaf. He was thought to have the makings of a responsible leader. Optimists believed that if Iraq were given a little more understanding and encouragement, it would become a more congenial neighbor.[45] Even in Israel, one of the most moderate members of the Knesset (the Israeli parliament), Abba Eban, pointed to the "reformed Saddam of Iraq."[46] Yet another group had felt all along that he would soon return to the policies that had characterized his regime before the war. They warned that Saddam was an "artful dodger." He had in fact been reinstating his practice of razing Kurdish villages and interfering in the affairs of Lebanon. Despite these solitary voices crying in the wilderness, the Americans and the British—and they were who really counted from then on—felt that he had changed for the better.

There were at least five main signals Saddam had given of his true intentions regarding the Arabs and the Middle East. The first clue was a speech on Jordanian television during a meeting of the Arab Cooperation Council on February 24, 1990.[47] In this speech, he spoke out against the United States and its policies in the Gulf. He stated that eventually the United States would take over the Gulf to satisfy its own needs; what was always at stake, he said, was oil, and it was time for the Arabs to do something about that. The speech ought to have given the West some pause—but it went unnoticed.

A second signal came on April 2 of that year. In a grand, public-affairs spectacle, Saddam announced that Iraqi scientists had developed more advanced chemical weapons, saying, "By God, we will make the fire eat up half of Israel, if it tries to do anything against Iraq."[48] The U.S. State Department called the threat "inflammatory, outrageous, irresponsible,"[49] but it said nothing more. Israel, of course, responded by threatening a nuclear strike if Iraq attacked it with chemical weapons. After that, Saddam's comments were simply dismissed. Israel was clearly worried, and Britain seemed no less anxious when Saddam attempted to smuggle huge steel pipes out of the United Kingdom for a long-range gun that was being produced. The Americans put Saddam's comments down to "defensive bluster" showing him fearful of an Israeli attack.[50] The Americans seemed unwilling to criticize Saddam directly. The third signal followed on May 28 at an Arab League summit meeting in Baghdad, where Saddam denounced the Arab states for keeping the oil prices too low. He stated in no uncertain terms that he considered this practice to be an "economic war" against Iraq, and he declared that he would not stand for it. Again, the Americans and British ignored the threats.

The fourth signal followed on July 17 during Hussein's Revolution Day speech in which he launched into a verbal attack against Kuwait and the United Arab Emirates over their oil policies. He indicated that he had sent a list of grievances to the Arab League about Kuwait. He accused Kuwait and the UAE of being part of "an imperialist-Zionist plot against the Arab nation."[51] Commenting on this, in its July 21 issue, the *Economist* stated that this sounded "alarmingly like a pretext for invasion."[52]

The final signal that clearly illuminated Iraq's intentions in the Gulf was sent out on July 24 when two Iraqi armored divisions were moved into position on the Kuwaiti border. On the twenty-fifth, the Canadian-born U.S. ambassador to Iraq, April Glaspie, was summoned to a meeting with Saddam. With no authority to do so, she stated that the United States would take no sides in the border dispute. This whole interview was perceived by Saddam as a sign of U.S. weakness. Glaspie did not take any measure to warn the Iraqi leader about the possible implications an Iraqi attack might have on Kuwait, and she did not alert him to the consequences it would have for U.S.-Iraqi relations.[53] Glaspie's interview with Saddam was indicative of U.S. laxity, and it was one among many in a series of precipitating events leading to the Iraqi dictator's decision to invade his tiny southern neighbor.

Why did the Americans choose to ignore these warnings? Why did they do nothing when it must have been obvious that Saddam had not changed from the man who had so brazenly invaded Iran ten years before? The answer is an obvious one. During the war itself, the Americans found themselves in a position where they had to choose sides. Having cut off relations with Iraq in the mid-1970s, and having been subjected to the indignity of enduring a hostage crisis in Iran, they opted for the philosophy "The enemy of my enemy is my friend." United States policy was to select the lesser of two evils—in this case, Iraq. Washington could not do otherwise. The political philosophy behind U.S. actions at all times seems to serve the "higher cause" of national security, that is, to fight communist forces and defend democracy and freedom, to eradicate the communist bogey wherever the U.S. government suspected it might rear its ugly head. Lest we also forget, U.S. policy toward Iraq goes as far back as the 1963 Ba'athist coup. The U.S. administration was following that event very closely, for Baghdad had quit the Baghdad Pact in 1958. By 1963 the Iraqi communists were so strong that they might have seized power. So, many analysts make the claim today that it was the U.S. CIA that actually put the Ba'athists in power in order to keep the Iraqi communists from taking it.[54] It should be remembered that when Iraq invaded Iran, the Americans prevented a UN response condemning Iraq for the act in much the same way that a condemnation was in effect adopted by the United States and the United Nations when Iraq invaded Kuwait.[55]

These are clearly double standards. Why would the U.S. government do something like this? It is plain to see that U.S. administrations have been more considerate to those who do not threaten U.S. interests. For example, the Americans balked from pressing a UN condemnation of Iraq for invading Iran insofar as that policy would have helped Iran, a nation so clearly anti-American, judging from the way U.S. embassy workers were taken hostage in Teheran only ten years before. Kuwait, on the other hand, was a U.S. ally that provided Americans with vast amounts of oil; and to be a credible ally, one cannot allow one's trading partners to be sacrificed to a man who threatens the stability of the Gulf. Oddly enough, in condemning Saddam's move against Kuwait, there is another double standard: U.S. policy makers seem to have forgotten how not too long ago the U.S. government sent troops to Panama to oust a drug dealer, how Washington blatantly interfered in the politics of Nicaragua and sent the United States Navy to attempt an assassination of the Libyan leader, Muammar Qaddafi. Why did American officials play down the poison gas attacks of the Iraqis during the Iran-Iraq war? Why did Washington ignore Saddam's threats, or the fact that Iraq was perhaps only a few years, or months, away from achieving nuclear capabilities? That could easily be ascertained from U.S. satellite intelligence; doubtless the Bush administration must have known how close Saddam was to the ultimate weapon.

An example of this blindness in U.S. thinking also appears in scholarly print. In 1988, Frederick W. Axelgard published a book for the Center for Strategic and International Studies (CSIS) in Washington, D.C.; it was titled *A New Iraq? The Gulf War and Implications for U.S. Policy*. The preface to this study was solicited from and written by Hermann Frederick Eilts, former U.S. ambassador to Saudi Arabia and Egypt and later director of the Center for International Relations at Boston University. In the book Eilts mindlessly praises Axelgard and the latter's equally mindless pleas for a positive outlook toward Iraq. Axelgard emphasizes all the good things

Saddam Hussein did for the Shi'i and Kurdish minorities in Iraq. He points to such things as Hussein's attracting Shi'i members to the Ba'ath, channeling industrial development into the southern, Shi'i areas, symbolic religious gestures to the Shi'ites, economic development of Kurdish areas, and land reform. He states that these Shi'ites were more loyal to the Iraqi leadership than to their Iranian coreligionists during the eight-year war. Axelgard also believes the Kurds were so politically divided that they were not at all effective. Only briefly does he mention how Iraqi Shi'ites were being arrested, expelled, or murdered by Saddam's secret police. Nor does he mention the punishment meted out to Kurdish separatists, the harsh resettlement campaigns, the use of chemical weapons against the Kurds, against their children, including the razing of Kurdish villages, and the Turkish-Iraqi agreement that allowed either Turks or Iraqis to pursue Kurdish rebels into each other's territory. The impression one gets from Axelgard's analysis is that Saddam was essentially compelled to do what he did and that the Shi'ites and Kurds got what they deserved.[56] How an informed author could ignore the murder of innocent women and children and the use of terrorist tactics by a government on its own people is absolutely reprehensible.

The center for which Axelgard works (CSIS) a U.S. "think tank," which, with the exception perhaps of Walter Laquer in its Asian, Soviet, and Middle East section, is known in the U.S. capital for its pervasive mediocrity. Consider a sample of Axelgard's writing: "Might not this leadership exert a lasting, stabilizing influence on Iraq and lift it out of its condition of perpetual tenuousness into the vitality of a full-fledged nation-state?"[57] Toward the end of the book, Axelgard gives both a summation of the Iraqi regime and a telling prognosis: "Saddam Hussein has injected moderation and pragmatism into a wide range of his external policies, from relations with the superpowers and the conservative Arab states of the Gulf to gestures of restraint and acceptance on the Arab-Israeli conflict"[58] and "after 40 years of volatility, realism may yet spawn a sustainable U.S. policy toward Iraq."[59]

This is not to say that Axelgard's analyses were carefully weighted as a determining factor in the minds of U.S. policy makers, but there was a minimal acceptance of this thesis by Washington. How could the U.S. Government, staffed with some of the most brilliant political minds in the world, allow itself to follow such a policy prescription?

The answer, disturbingly enough, seems to come down to bare economics. Ever since the reestablishment of ties between the United States and Iraq in 1984, Iraq became the largest importer of U.S. rice and wheat. Not surprisingly, an unofficial, pro-Iraqi lobby operated in Washington; its purpose was to keep relations between the two countries on a sound footing. In fact, at the height of the Gulf crisis, several representatives of U.S. wheat and rice farmers made a strong bid to prevent the imposition of sanctions against Iraq following its invasion of Iran. At one point, before Saddam's attack on Kuwait (April 12, 1990), a group of five U.S. senators led by Robert Dole visited Saddam Hussein in Baghdad. Ostensibly sent there to reprimand him for his policies, the group actually ended up flattering him. One of the senators "told Mr. Hussein that the "Voice of America" journalist responsible for criticizing Iraq's secret police had been sacked."[60] They blamed most of Iraq's image problem in the West on the U.S. press. Afterwards, John Kelly, the State Department's undersecretary for Middle East affairs, fought congressional moves to impose economic sanctions on Iraq, arguing that sanctions would "impair the administration's ability to exert 'a restraining influence.' "[61] As little as a week before the invasion, Kelly was making this very same assertion.

The U.S. has thus profited from its relationship with Iraq. Washington sold Saddam weapons and supplies and gave away vital spy-satellite information during the war with Iran. Americans received billions of dollars worth of oil and traded vast amounts of goods with the Iraqis, all at an enormous profit. United States businesspeople and arms merchants set the tone for a pro-Iraqi attitude in the United States. But the Europeans are also to blame: The Soviets sold Iraq the bulk of the arms and armor; the French supplied him with Exocet missiles and Mirage fighter planes; the Germans supplied technology for chemical and bacteriological warfare, and German engineers helped lace the Iraqi army's bunkers with state-of-the-art reinforced steel, producing an impregnability that was the envy of the NATO forces. The transfer of this war-making technology was absolutely illegal under COCOM (Coordinating Committee on Multilateral Export Controls) regulations. The public in the West realized this only when war broke out between the U.S.-led coalition and the Iraqi regime in January of 1991. As Kendal Nezan of the Kurdish Institute in Paris stated in connection with the treatment of the Kurds under Saddam Hussein: "We have been crying out in the desert about the extremely evil character of the regime....We weren't heard because of a wall of mercantile interests. As a result, a tinhorn dictator has now become a monster."[62] How ironic, then, for the United States to be blustering about the illegality of Iraq's actions, to go to war to destroy Saddam's regime, when the U.S. government, albeit unwittingly, had a hand in keeping Saddam in power.

But there is yet another irony. In spite of the official condemnations of Saddam's action by the governments of nearly every Middle Eastern country, most of the people of these countries see Hussein as an Arab nationalist hero. Eye-witness reports reflected on the mood of the Arab people. "Not since Nasser had an Arab leader uttered such chilling, and chillingly plausible, threats against Israel. Arabs everywhere are thrilled."[63] If anything, Saddam had proved to most Arabs that they could face down the Americans. Since the Arabs had suffered such humiliating defeats in the three latest wars in the region (1948, 1967, and 1973), they saw in the ruler of Iraq another—though the comparison is, of course, ludicrous—Saladin, the only "Arab" (Saladin himself was not an Arab) capable of rallying the people and driving the marauding crusaders (in this case the Americans, the West, and Israel) from their shores.

Saddam Hussein hinted on several occasions that if he could keep the Rumaila oilfield and the islands of Warba and Bubiyan, which control Iraq's access to the Gulf, he might withdraw from the rest of Kuwait. Yevgeny Primakov, an aide to Mikhail Gorbachev, floated such proposals to President George Bush.[64] But the U.S. president's agenda was first to restore Kuwait to the *status quo ante*. The deeper, more significant agenda was to destroy Saddam and his regime before that regime could do any damage to the Middle East with an arsenal of nuclear weapons. On this score, the U.S. president entered into a private understanding with Saudi Arabia's King Fahd, Egypt's Hosni Mubarak, and Syria's Hafez el-Assad. The diplomatic solution receded further and further into the background as Saddam was given an ultimatum by the U.S. Security Council to withdraw from Kuwait by January 15, 1991—the ultimate deadline. As some U.S. analysts observed: "If Saddam's annexation of Kuwait were permitted to stand, Washington reasoned, wholesale disavowals of old colonial borders and land grabs throughout the Middle East might become commonplace."[65] If the United States failed to rid the world of Saddam Hussein, the world, Iraq's neighbors, including Israel, might have to contend with Saddam sometime in the future. If Saddam had withdrawn from Kuwait before the January 15 deadline, he would not have lost face before the Arab world; he would have kept his forces intact to fight another day—next time stronger, richer, brandishing in the next round a possible nuclear clout.

When the war against Saddam erupted, Western military analysts hoped and were proven correct in their assumptions that it would be short. They also hoped that it would eliminate Saddam's regime. But the military men seemed to overlook the possibility that after Saddam's war there might be a power vacuum for a considerable period of time, although they did observe that Iraq served as the balance between Israel and sixty million Persians.[66] Others in the West, well disposed to Saddam and Iraqi power argued that there was no alternative to Saddam Hussein. They correctly predicted that Iraqi Shi'ites might clamor for a separate republic, backed by Shi'i Iran. This is exactly what happened. Yahya Sadowski of the Brookings Institution even expressed the fear that the Kurds might likewise wish to establish a separate republic. She warned that the Kurds were led by radicals and reminded us that they were concentrated near Iraq's northern oilfields. "Do we want a Kurdish state in OPEC?" she asked.[67] Others worried that Turkey could also make a bid for that old Ottoman administrative district of Mosul, so rich in oil. And what about the hopes for a Palestinian national state; were these hopes and dreams to be dashed if Saddam failed?

Militarily, the Americans could not lose the war and Saddam could not win it. Politically, if the war had been drawn out over many months the Americans would have lost a great deal of prestige, which would have meant Saddam's game—even if Saddam had not survived it. The fallout on the Arab world would have been devastating. And where would the Great Game have gone from there? As it turned out, Saddam lost the war in six weeks, and in his humiliation and defeat, with practically the entire Iraqi infrastructure in ruins, he failed to project the appeal to the Arabs that he hoped.[68]

NOTES

1. Samir al-Khalil, *Republic of Fear: The Politics of Modern Iraq* (Los Angeles: University of California Press, 1989), 219. Samir al-Khalil is a pseudonym to protect family members still in Iraq.

2. Ibid.

3. Quoted by al-Khalil, *Republic of Fear*, 122.

4. The southern terminal of the East India Company's overland mail route to Aleppo (Syria) was moved from Basra to Kuwait, and much of the trade of Basra was diverted to Kuwait.

5. Stephen Pelletiere, *The Kurds: An Unstable Element in the Gulf* (Boulder, Colo.: Westview Press, 1984), 23.

6. Both are Aryans, speaking a language of the Indo-European group, though the two languages are not mutually intelligible.

7. Before World War I Iraq was part of the Ottoman Empire; it was not yet a state. In the interwar period it was a British mandate. The territory was rich in oil and had one of the largest concentration of Kurds. On October 3, 1932, Iraq was admitted as an independent state to the League of Nations.

8. Pelletiere, *The Kurds*, 32ff.

9. Ibid., 33.

10. Ibid., 34.

11. Carl Brown, *International Politics in the Middle East* (Princeton, N.J.: Princeton University Press, 1984). See the introductory chapter in particular.

12. Cited in Pelletiere, *The Kurds*, 57. Also see Edmund Ghareeb, *The Kurdish Question in Iraq* (Syracuse, N.Y.: Syracuse University Press, 1981), pp. 6–7.

13. Jasmir M. Abdulghani, *Iraq & Iran: The Years of Crisis* (London: Croom Helm, 1984).

14. For an overview of the rise and demise of the Mahabad Republic, see Pelletiere, *The Kurds*, 99–114. See also Ghareeb, *The Kurdish Question*, 11–12.

15. Pelletiere, *The Kurds*, 116.

16. Ghareeb, *The Kurdish Question*, 38.

17. Pelletiere, *The Kurds*, 126.

18. Ibid., 129.

19. Cited in Abdulghani, *Iraq & Iran: the Years of Crisis*, 133.

20. Pelletiere, *The Kurds*, 164.

21. Ghareeb, *The Kurdish Question*, 76.

22. Cited in ibid., 108.

23. See Abdulghani, *Iraq & Iran: The Years of Crisis*, 137–138.

24. *New York Times*, April 1, 1974. The extent of the Iranian, U.S., and Israeli involvement with Barzani has been extensively documented. See Abdulghani, *Iraq & Iran: The Years of Crisis*, 139–147; and Ghareeb, *The Kurdish Question*, 131–146.

25. For a penetrating analysis of the U.S. role, see Pelletiere, *The Kurds*, 167–176.

26. Ibid., 169.

27. Ibid., 179. Pelletiere adds that "in specific instances [Barzani] may even have cooperated with Savak" to achieve the suppression of the Iranian Kurdish movement. Ghareeb points out that "the leadership of the Iranian KDP differ markedly from that of the Iraq KDP. While the Barzani leadership depended on tribal loyalty, the Iranian leadership depended on intellectuals and enjoyed the backing of urban dwellers and peasants" (p. 14).

28. Ibid., 183.

29. Ibid., 184.

30. Ibid., 187.

31. Ibid.

32. Ibid. There are widely varying estimates of the Kurdish populations and their distribution across countries. Pelletiere estimates there to be 7 million to 7.5 million Kurds. D. A. Schmidt, *New York Times* reporter, estimates around 2 million Kurds in Iraq, 4–5 million in Turkey, 3 million in Iran, around 300,000 in Syria, and about 175,000 in the USSR—around 10 million all told. These are considered conservative estimates. In a *New York Times* article (May 17, 1987), Alan Cowell estimated the numbers to be 3.5 million in Iraq ("one-quarter of the population"), 5.5 million in Iran, and 8–10 million in Turkey. Part of the problem lies in establishing precise ethnic identities in the areas in question.

33. "Opposition Regroups," *Afkar-Inquiry*, February 1987, p. 9.

34. Ibid., 8.

35. Ibid.

36. Ibid., 7.

37. Ibid.

38. Zubaida Umar, "The Forgotten Minority: The Turkomans of Iraq," *Afkar-Inquiry*, February 1987, p. 37.

39. *Kayhan*, November 1, 1986, p. 1.

40. *Economist*, January 17, 1987, p. 54.

41. *New Republic*, May, 1988.

42. Ibid. The best account of the destruction of "Osirak" is contained in Dan McKinnon's *Bullseye Iraq* (New York: Berkeley Books, 1988). Peter Galbraith, a staff member of the Senate Foreign Relations Committee in the United States, had visited the Kurdish area of Iraq in 1987. He wrote:

Village after village had been destroyed.... The place had a kind of eerie silence and beauty, but what had once been an area filled with villages and life and some 2 million people was suddenly empty The Kurdish villages that had been there almost since the beginning of time were gone. Their inhabitants had been moved to concentration camps erected hastily around a few major towns.

Quoted by Judith Miller and Laurie Mylroie in *Saddam Hussein and the Crisis in the Gulf* (New York: Times Books–Random House, 1990), 147–148.

43. *Time*, August 13, 1990, p. 12.

44. *Time*, August 27, 1990, p. 19.

45. *Economist*, August 4, 1990, p. 33.

46. *Yediot Aharonot*, June 2, 1990.

47. *Economist*, September 29, 1990.

48. Ibid., 20.

49. Ibid.

50. *Newsweek*, July 2, 1990, p. 29.

51. Ibid., 22.

52. Ibid.

53. Ibid. The transcript of the meeting between Saddam Hussein and Ambassador Glaspie of the United States was released by the government of Iraq and published by the *New York Times* on September 23, 1990. The U.S. State Department refused to confirm or deny its validity.

54. Fred Halliday, "Biting the Western Hand That Helped Them," *Manchester Guardian Weekly*, August 19, 1990, p. 7.

55. Ibid.

56. Axelgard pays scant attention to Saddam Hussein's practice of abducting and torturing the children of Iraqi Kurdish families. For a good account of Iraqi torture practices, see *Human Rights in Iraq by the Middle East Watch*, published by the Human Rights Watch (New Haven, Conn.: Yale University Press, November 1990). Widespread abuses of human rights were perpetrated by Iraqi troops in Kuwait. They tortured and killed hundreds of people; thousands more were imprisoned, and in one instance three hundred premature babies were removed from their incubators and left to die on hospital floors. The incubators were carted off to Iraq. See *Amnesty International Report*, December 18, 1990. It is also noteworthy that in a book written by Stephen C. Pelletiere, Lt. Col. Douglas V. Johnson II, and Leif R. Rosenberger, *Iraqi Power and U.S. Security in the Middle East* (Carlisle Barracks, Pennsylvania: Strategic Studies Institute, U.S. Army War College, 1989, 95 pp.), the authors actually questioned whether Iraq had used chemicals against the Kurdish population and criticized George Schultz and the U.S. Senate for seeking to impose sanctions on Iraq after the gas attacks. The authors even assert that it was the Iranians' gas that killed the Kurds at Halabja. The reader will note that the writers of this fatuous account are employed by the U.S. Army War College in Pennsylvania. For a debate on this subject between the writers above and Edward Mortimer, a British journalist working for the *Financial Times* and author of *Faith and Power* (one of the best books written on Islam and politics), see the *New York Review of Books*, November 22, 1990.

57. Frederick W. Axelgard, *A New Iraq? The Gulf War and Implications for U.S. Policy* (New York: Praeger and Washington, D.C.: Center for Strategic and International Studies, 1988), 47–48.

58. Ibid., 91.

59. Ibid., 103. The French defense minister, Jean-Pierre Chevènement, was probably the first public official anywhere who set this tone. Chevènement had founded an Iraqi-French friendship society. He quit his post in the French government when war erupted in the Gulf; he was chastised in the French press for having praised Saddam so often in the past.

60. *Economist*, September 29, 1990, p. 20.

61. Ibid., 20–21. For an interesting corroborative account, see James Price, *Back-*

ground to the Gulf Crisis: The U.S.-Iraqi Rapprochement, Unpublished paper, September 1990. James Prince is a legislative assistant to U.S. congressman Matthew Martinez. The article, one of the first that I have read, effectively blames the entire Reagan administration for its short-sighted policies on Iraq.

62. *Newsweek*, August 20, 1990, p. 29.

63. *Economist*, September 29, 1990, p. 19.

64. *Newsweek*, October 29, 1990.

65. Miller and Mylroie, *Saddam Hussein*, 229.

66. *Newsweek*, October 29, 1990.

67. Ibid.

68. The present book does not give an account of the war itself. For an account of the war, see my book on Saddam Hussein's wars, forthcoming in 1992. Also see Miron Rezun, *Post-Khomeini Iran and the New Gulf War*, CQRI monograph, Laval University, Quebec City, 1991.

7

Epilogue

It is often said that the most important chapter in a book is the concluding one. As the author of this imperfect book, I submit that many will turn to the last chapter, looking for a clue to the rest and skipping everything that comes between the Introduction and the Conclusion. This epilogue, however, is meant to serve neither as a conclusion nor as a summing-up: It is a continuation of arguments left in abeyance or unanswered thus far. Perhaps for this reason the last chapter carries a punch that is absent in all the preceding ones. If readers are still unsatisfied, if they find a paucity of explanations here, they need only go back and dwell a little longer on the chapter narratives that discuss the intricacies of the Great Game in greater detail.

This said, I must again invoke the major focus of my theme in this book: that there are underlying realities, hidden agendas, and hidden ambitions that often escape us when we undertake the study of conflict and war. Barring some hidden plan of nature, the realities of international politics are intimately linked to the underlying facts and underlying interests. Sometimes these interests are common, international interests; sometimes they are not, for they may be wholly selfish interests. And there is more in these realities than meets the eye; or to revert to a currently fashionable assumption, reality is something *less* than meets the eye. This easily leads to a frightening picture of the world politics where federative leagues and organizations, like the United Nations, may never be able to achieve lasting peace as long as states behave as they have customarily behaved. "Politics," Albert Einstein once noted, "is much harder than physics." It is the politics in each instance in the struggles of Southwest Asia that has led to conflict and war. War, in turn, is subordinated to politics. This is essentially a maxim that had once been coined by the Prussian philosopher-soldier-strategist Karl von Clausewitz. Politics, or cunning politicking, begins again when the war comes to an end and peace and a new order is sought after.

The Clausewitzian analysis in effect holds some optimism for the future: Given that they are a continuation of politics, all wars will end if fought for political reasons—unless, of course, these wars are inherently struggles of life and death, fought out of pure hatred. In the context of the Great Game in Southwest Asia, the history of the region to this very day indicates that these wars have not been life-and-death struggles; they have been fought for concrete political or economic motives. Indeed, foreign powers have interfered in this region for particular stakes, whether out of self-interest or otherwise. But if the history of this region tells us anything, it is that Clausewitz's optimism in all probability will not be borne out the way he had expected. It would, moreover, be difficult to be optimistic about this region, to say the least. Old realities have simply given way to new ones, and an intricate international game of intrigue begins anew.

Also, it is exceedingly difficult to attain an objective truth in describing the events of a region that is so conflict-ridden, so disparate in its ethnic mosaic, so dependent on foreign elements. Even historians, writing about this subject many years hence, will be trapped by the fallacies of their own prevailing logic. We are reminded of David Hackett Fischer's verdict when he poked fun at the radical, modern historians of his day "who regard all aspirations to objectivity as a sham and a humbug, and stubbornly insist that the real question is not whether historians can be objective, but which cause they will be subjective to."[1]

But why all this skepticism about contemporary Southwest Asia? Am I being overly obsequious to the tyranny of what I have perceived as the Great Game?

Let me say at the very outset that this Great Game will likely continue, despite the need for what President Bush has called a "new international world order." Such a "new order" could only be peace proposals and peace settlements set up according to the whims and interests of the U.S. government alone. In this scenario, the United Nations would never emerge as an even-handed policeman in global affairs. If that were the case, the Western world would fall silent and remain supportive of U.S. policies. The reality is that the United Nations, in and of itself, is too weak to execute policies anywhere in the world. When an agreement came about on a withdrawal by Soviet forces from Afghanistan, it was made only under UN auspices; the whole thing was drummed up as a U.S.-Soviet entente, and that has still not ended the murderous war in Afghanistan. Moreover, if the United Nations had not given a mandate to a U.S.-led coalition to respond to Saddam Hussein's seizure of Kuwait, the Americans would have intervened as they did anyway with half a million troops and obtained European support for their actions. The United States alone in the world will continue to act as if it can morally and legally determine the punishment that will fit any crime, a punishment meted out and tailored to whomever and whatever is at stake. After all, did Saddam Hussein not ask why the world waged a war to enforce a UN resolution when that same organization would not contemplate war to enforce much older UN resolutions that Israel must leave the West Bank and the Gaza Strip?

During the war in the Gulf that pitted Iraq against the coalition, Saddam Hussein attempted to link a settlement with the Israeli-Palestinian issue. He failed, of course. But the West is divided on how to proceed. The Europeans, including the British, would like to convene an international conference to which the Soviet Union would be invited together with the Palestinians. But which Palestinians? The PLO's support for Iraq during the war has cost it dearly. The United States and Israel have ruled out dealing with Yassir Arafat as long as he represents the leadership of the Palestinians. Surely, the issue of the future of the Palestinian people is the single most important concern of the Great Powers and no doubt will top the international agenda for years to come. Yet no one thus far has even cared to raise the question of another stateless people—the Kurds. The united opposition of all the neighboring countries, particularly Turkey—we must be mindful that U.S. policies are sensitive to Turkey's position as a member of NATO—to the creation of an independent Kurdish state is an important factor against the Kurds' chances of breaking away from Iraq. An independent Kurdistan in northern Iraq may very well lead to unrest among the Turkish Kurds, whose population inside Turkey is probably around fifteen million. Turkey has stated on numerous occasions that it would intervene to prevent the establishment of a neighboring Kurdish state.

This has certainly not prevented the Turks from keenly scrutinizing recent developments in Soviet Azerbaijan and in Soviet Turkestan. When Ankara is not watching what the Kurds are up to, or trying by hook or by crook to get into the European Community, it follows with great intensity the struggle between the Armenians and the Azeri Turks in Transcaucasia. Now that the war has ended in the Gulf and civil war is raging in Iraq itself, Turkey is hungrily coveting those areas of northern Iraq that at the time of the Ottoman Empire belonged to Turkey: the oil-rich areas of Iraqi Kurdistan.

In the aftermath of the second Gulf War, the United States is prepared to establish a new basis for peace. But that basis will not include a new order or a new framework; it must build on the old one by enlarging and strengthening the GCC, the regional economic grouping led by Saudi Arabia that includes Kuwait and the rest of the Gulf states. Egypt and Syria, former allies in the U.S.-led coalition—how strange that Ba'athist Syria, with hands steeped in blood, should parley with the United States on equal terms about a postwar peace—are not linked to the GCC, playing a vital role in the future of the region's security. While this is taking place it should not be surprising to witness a falling out between Syria and Iran, friends during the Iran-Iraq war, but states with different stakes in the Gulf now that Syria will aspire, together with Egypt, to lead the Arab world. How ironic that Syria now runs Lebanon, with Washington's blessings, just the way Iraq wanted to run Kuwait, except that the Americans would not let it. The only good thing to come of the Gulf War is perhaps that Kuwait, damaged and ravished in every way, especially in terms of its infrastructure, by atrocities and by environmental pollution, will hold parliamentary elections within a year.

There are other ironies, too. When Iraq began to use internationally outlawed chemical weapons to slaughter waves of Iranian teenagers in 1984, Western chancelleries were silent. In 1987, when Iraq fired more than 100 Scud missiles at Teheran and other Iranian cities, there was no Western condemnation of what U.S. president George Bush later called a weapon of terror when the Scuds landed in Israel and Saudi Arabia during the last Gulf War. It is strange that the media treated the last Gulf War almost as a major war, in view of the large numbers of Americans participating in it. When Saddam Hussein had gassed nearly five thousand of his own Kurds at Halabja in March 1988, the Western powers (and the media as well) did not specifically condemn this Iraqi atrocity until Saddam Hussein threatened to use chemical weapons against the Allies in Saudi Arabia.

A *Pax Americana* imposed by the United States in the Gulf region that excluded the Soviet Union could turn Arab public opinion against the West. President Mikhail Gorbachev tried to mollify his right wing and the Soviet military, who were saying that the USSR had gone too far in siding with the United States and the West against Iraq. The Soviet military budget was being reduced, the Warsaw Pact was being dissolved, and the Red Army in Europe was already becoming redundant. The *New York Times* observed the Soviet generals' anger: "The growls came instinctively when the adversary of 40 years unsheathed new weapons within a cannon shot of Soviet land, and an arms client of long standing came under threat from NATO."[2] The performance of U.S. high-technology weapons, particularly in the air assault on Iraq's military superstructure, has Soviet military planners worried about the lack of sophistication regarding the Soviet military clout. The Stealth fighter and the American sea-launched cruise missiles simply do not have a Soviet equivalent.

Furthermore, many Soviet Moslems see Hussein as a defender of the faith. Some Moslem leaders agitated against the U.S. and the coalition and this led to demonstrations against Bush and Zionism in Moscow on January 19th. Even the Supreme Soviet of the different Moslem republics could not agree on how to act. The Supreme Soviet of Kirgizia wrote letters to the embassies of the Americans, Kuwaitis, and Saudis in Moscow asking them to cease hostilities. Uzbekistan's Supreme Soviet appealed to Gorbachev to stop the conflict. The Supreme Soviet of Azerbaijan said that the war went beyond the U.N. mandate and simply stated that the liberation of Kuwait was only a pretext to protect American oil interests. Later in February, several Moscow newspapers reported that the Iraqi embassy had received over ten thousand letters from Soviet citizens, most of whom were Moslem, volunteering to fight for Iraq.[3]

Gorbachev thus tried to appease his generals as well as his own restive Moslem population, which sympathizes with Moslem brethren everywhere. Shortly afterwards, when Gorbachev held a referendum on a new Union of the Soviet Empire, the Moslems, more than anyone else, gave him their full support, and therefore it is reasonable for the USSR to argue that it cannot be denied a permanent interest in Southwest Asia and the Middle East.

All the region's fundamental problems remain: states armed to the hilt and artificial borders imposed by colonial powers who are gone but come back to meddle in the affairs of the regional powers. For a regional power to be successful in its policies, it must have the full support of a superpower—and thus far that superpower appears to be the United States, not the Soviet Union in decline. There are gaping disparities between the fabulously wealthy few and the dirt-poor majority (note that only 20 percent of the population of Kuwait has the right to vote); scarce resources like oil and water are unevenly distributed; there are still governments that range from effete, semifeudal monarchies to brutal dictatorships.

The Game is an old one with recurring patterns. The main feature is hence the desire of smaller players to use regional conflicts and the superpowers to promote their own interests. Another feature is the double standards the superpowers (the United States and the USSR) use in advancing their own interests. Caught in the middle of the "Game," of course, are innocent human beings who, both as players and non-players, end up in a "zero-sum" equation. The needless sufferings of the Kurds and Afghans are a case in point.

The moment Saddam Hussein falls from power, a tremendous void will be created in Iraq, with all the regional powers, and the superpowers, moving in to fill it. Possibly the country to watch carefully from now on is Iran.[4] In Teheran, the emigre Shi'i cleric Ayatollah Bakr Hakim has intensified his campaign to rouse the Iraqi Shi'ites to establish an Islamic Republic in Iraq. Rafsanjani has already said that he expects Saddam to be ousted and has expressed disgust over the massacre of Shi'ites in the south and the Kurds in the north by Iraq's Republican Guard during the aftermath of the Gulf War.

NOTES

1. David Hackett Fischer, *Historians' Fallacies: Toward a Logic of Historical Thought* (New York: Harper and Row Publishers, 1970), 314.

2. *New York Times*, March 10, 1991.

3. George Stein, "Soviet Muslims Divided on Gulf War" in *Radio Liberty—Report on the USSR* 3, no. 8, February 22, 1991, p. 13.

4. For more details, see my book *Post-Khomeini Iran and the New Gulf War* (in French and English) (Quebec City: Centre Québécois de Relations Internationales, Laval University, 1991).

Selected Bibliography

SELECTED ARTICLES

Bennigsen, Alexandre. "Minorités musulmanes en URSS." *Projet*, no. 147 (1980).
Bennigsen, Alexandre. "Soviet Muslims and the World of Islam." *Problems of Communism* 29, no. 2 (1980).
Bohr, Annette. "Turkmenistan under Perestroika: An Overview." Radio Liberty, *Report on the USSR* (Munich), February 16, 1990.
Chokayev, Mustafa. "The Basmachi Movement in Turkestan." *Asiatic Review* 24, no. 4 (1928).
Critchlow, James. "Uzbeks Demand Halt to Russian In-Migration." Radio Liberty, *Report on the USSR* (Munich), March 2, 1990.
Fraser, Glenda. "Haji Sami and the Turkestan Federation." *Asian Affairs* 28, no. 1 (1987).
Globe, Paul. "Central Asians Form Political Bloc." Radio Liberty, *Report on the USSR* (Munich), July 13, 1990.
Hauner, Milan. "The USSR and the Indo-Persian Corridor." *Problems of Communism*, no. 1 (January–February 1987).
Khalilzad, Zalmay. "The War in Afghanistan." *International Journal* 4, no. 2 (1986).
Kuttner, Thomas. "Russian Jadidism and the Islamic World." *Cahiers du Monde russe et soviétique* 3–4, no. 16 (34) (July-December 1975).
Naby, Eden. "Tajiks Reemphasize Iranian Heritage as Ethnic Pressures Mount in Central Asia." Radio Liberty, *Report on the USSR* (Munich), February 16, 1990.
Rezun, Miron. "Afghanistan's Twists." *International Perspectives*, no. 7 (March 1989).

———. "Reza Shah's Court Minister: Teymourtash." *International Journal of Middle Eastern Studies*, no. 12 (1980).

———. "The Soviet Moslems: A Re-assessment." *Middle East Focus* 9, no. 4 (Spring 1987).

Ro'i, Yaacov. "The Islamic Influence on Nationalism in Soviet Central Asia." *Problems of Communism* 31, no. 4 (July-August, 1990).

Rorlich, Azade-Ayse. "The Disappearance of an Old Taboo: Is Sultangaliev Becoming Persona Grata?" Radio Liberty, *Report on the USSR* (Munich), September 29, 1989.

———. "Fellow Travellers: Enver Pasha and the Bolshevik Government, 1918–1920." *Asian Affairs* 13, no. 3 (1982).

Saroyan, Mark. "The 'Karabakh Syndrome' and Azerbaijani Politics." *Problems of Communism* 39, no. 5 (September-October 1990).

Sick, Gary. "Iran's Quest for Superpower Status." *Foreign Affairs* 65, no. 4 (Spring 1987).

Umar, Zubaida. "The Forgotten Minority: The Turkomans of Iraq." *Afkar-Inquiry*, (February 1987).

Yapp, M. E. "Contemporary Islamic Revival." *Asian Affairs*, (1980).

BOOKS

Akiner, Shirin. "Uzbeks." In *The Nationalities Question in the Soviet Union*, ed. Graham Smith. Essex, England: Longman Group, 1990.

Alger, Hamid, trans. *Constitution of the Islamic Republic of Iran*. Berkeley, Calif.: Mizan Press, 1980.

al-Khalil, Samil. *Republic of Fear: The Politics of Modern Iraq*. Los Angeles: University of California Press, 1989.

Alleg, Henri. *Etoile Rouge et Croissant Vert* (Red Star and green crescent). Paris: Temps Actuels, 1983.

Bennigsen, Alexandre, and Marie Broxup. *The Islamic Threat to the Soviet State*. New York: St. Martin's Press, 1983.

Bennigsen, Alexandre, and S. Enders Wimbush. *Muslim National Communism in the Soviet Union: A Revolutionary Strategy for the Colonial World*. Chicago: University of Chicago Press, 1979.

Blank, Stephen. " 'Glastnost' and Afghanistan." In *Glasnost, Perestroika and the Socialist Community*, ed. Charles Bukowski and J. Richard Walsh. New York: Praeger, 1990.

Bradsher, Henry. *The Soviet Union and Afghanistan*. Durham, N.C.: Duke University Press, 1983.

Brown, Carl. *International Politics in the Middle East*. Princeton: Princeton University Press, 1984.

Bulloch, John, and Harvey Morris. *Saddam's War*. London: Faber and Faber, 1991.

Caroe, Olaf. *Soviet Empire: The Turks of Central Asia and Stalinism*. London: MacMillan and Co., 1953.

Castagne, Joseph. *Les Basmatchis* (The Basmachi). Paris: Editions Leroux, 1925.

Chomsky, Noam. *The Culture of Terrorism*. Montreal: Black Rose Books, 1988.

Cordesmann, Anthony. *The Persian Gulf and the West*. Boulder, Colo.: Westview Press, 1987.

Darwish, Adel, and Gregory Alexander. *Unholy Babylon*. London: Gollancz, 1991.

d'Encausse, Hélène Carrère. *Reforme et Revolution chez les Musulmans de l'Empire Russe: Bukhara, 1867–1924*. (Reform and revolution among Muslims of the Roman Empire). Paris: Armand Colin, 1966.

Feshbach, M., and S. Rapawy. "Soviet Population and Manpower Trends and Policies." In *Soviet Economy in a New Perspective*. Washington: Joint Economic Committee, U.S. Congress, 1976.

Ghareeb, Edmund. *The Kurdish Question in Iraq*. Syracuse: Syracuse University Press, 1981.

Glasneck, Johannes, and Inge Kircheisen. *Turkei und Afghanistan: Brennpunkte der Orientpolitik in Zweiten Weltkreig* (Turkey and Afghanistan—Focal Points of Eastern Politics during World War II). East Berlin: Deutsche Staatsverlag, 1968.

Halliday, Fred. *Iran, Dictatorship and Development*. Middlesex: Penguin Books, 1979.

Klass, Roxanna, ed. *Afghanistan: The Great Game Revisited*. New York: Freedom House, 1987.

Lenin, V. I. *Sobranie Sochinienii* (collected works). Moscow: Politizdat, 1971.

McKinnon, Dan. *Bullseye Iraq*. New York: Berkley Books, 1987.

Miller, Judith, and Laurie Mylroie. *Saddam Hussein and the Crisis in the Gulf*. New York: Random House, 1990.

Millward, W. G. "The Principles of Foreign Policy and the Vision of World Order Expounded by Imam Khomeini and the Islamic Republic of Iran." In *The Iranian Revolution and the Islamic Repubic*, ed. Nikki R. Keddie and Eric Hooglund. Washington, D.C.: Yale University Press, 1982.

Pelletiere, Stephen. *The Kurds: An Unstable Element in the Gulf*. Boulder, Colo.: Westview Press, 1984.

Pelletiere, Stephen, Douglas Johnson II, and Leif Rosenberger. *Iraqi Power and U.S. Security in the Middle East*. Carlisle Barracks, Penn.: Strategic Studies Institute, 1990.

Price, James. *Background to the Gulf Crisis: The U.S.-Iraqi Rapprochement*. Unpublished paper, September 1990.

Rakowska-Harmstone, Teresa. *Russia and Nationalism in Central Asia*. Baltimore: Johns Hopkins Press, 1970.

Ramazani, R. K. "Khomeini's Islam in Iran's Foreign Policy." In *Islam in Foreign Policy*, ed. K. Dawisha. New York: Cambridge University Press, 1983.

Rasiak, Rusian O. "The Soviet People: Multiethnic Alternative or Ruse?" In *Ethnic Russia in the USSR*, ed. Edward Allworth. New York: Pergamon Press, 1980.

Rezun, Miron. *Iran at the Crossroads*. Boulder, Colo.: Westview Press, 1990.

———. *Post-Khomeini Iran and the New Gulf War*. Quebec: CQRI monograph, 1991.

———. *The Soviet Union and Iran*. Boulder, Colo.: Westview Press, 1988.

Rothman, Stanley, and George Breslauer. *Soviet Politics and Society*. St. Paul: West Publishing Co., 1978.

Ryskulov, Turar. *Revoliutsia i Korennoe Naselenie Turkestana* (Revolution and the native population of Turkestan). Tashkent: Nauka, 1925.

Seraphim, H. G., ed. *Das Politische Tagebuch Alfred Rosenbergs, 1934–1935 und 1939–1940* (Alfred Rosenberg's political diary: 1934–1935 and 1939–1940). Munich: Deutscher Taschenbuch Verlag, 1964.

Yapp, Malcolm. "Soviet Relations with Countries of the Northern Tier" in *The Soviet*

Union in the Middle East, ed. Adeed Dawisha and Karen Dawisha. London: Heinemann, 1982.

Zevelev, A. I., L. A. Poliakov, and A. I. Chugunov. *Basmachestvo: Vozniknovenie, Sushchnost', Krakh* (Basmachism: Origin, essence, collapse). Moscow: Nauka, 1981.

DOCUMENTS

Documents on German Foreign Policy, 1918–1945

MAGAZINES

Afkar-Inquiry
Economist
Kayhan
MacLean's
Newsweek
Novaia Zemlya
Novyi Vostok
Time
Yediot Aharonot

NEWSPAPERS

San Francisco Chronicle
Globe and Mail
London Times
Los Angeles Times
Manchester Guardian Weekly
New York Times
Washington Post

Index

ABOUT THE AUTHOR

MIRON REZUN is Associate Professor of Political Science at the University of New Brunswick, Canada. He has published many books and articles about the Soviet Union and the Middle East. Current topics include nationalism in Central Asia and Azerbaijan, and a controversial study of Saddam Hussein, the Persian Gulf War, and U.S. policies in the Middle East.